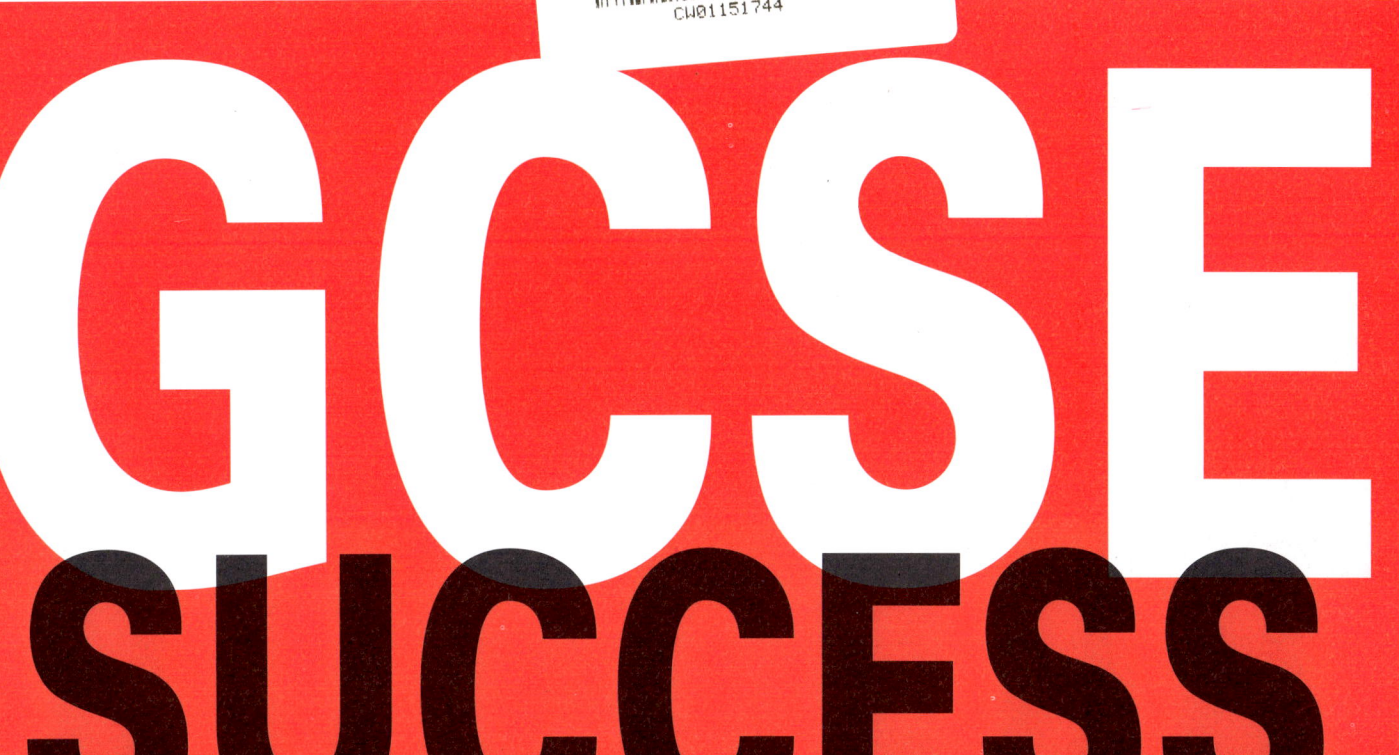

Letts

Revision Notes

CW01151744

GCSE SUCCESS

Science Higher

NEAB

Authors

John Dobson

Paul Levy

Brian McCullagh

Series editor

Alan Brewerton

Every effort has been made to trace copyright holders and to obtain their permission for the use of copyright material. The authors and publishers will gladly receive information enabling them to rectify any error or omission in subsequent editions.

First published 1998
This edition 1999

Letts Educational, 9–15 Aldine Street, London W12 8AW
Tel. 0208 740 2270
Fax 0208 740 2280

Text © John Dobson, Paul Levy and Brian McCullagh 1998

Editorial, design and production by Hart McLeod, Cambridge

All our rights reserved. No part of this publication may be reproduced, stored in a retrieval system, or transmitted, in any form or by any means, electronic, mechanical, photocopying, recording or otherwise, without prior permission of Letts Educational.

British Library Cataloguing-in-Publication Data
A CIP record for this book is available from the British Library

ISBN 1 84085 287 9

Printed and bound in Italy

Letts Educational is the trading name of BPP (Letts Educational) Ltd

The authors and publisher would like to thank St. David's School, Middlesbrough for their technical help and assistance with this project.

Contents

Life processes and living things

Life processes and cell activity	6
Humans as organisms	9
Green plants as organisms	18
Variation, inheritance and evolution	24
Living things and their environment	30

Materials and their properties

Classifying materials and considering reactions	37
Patterns of behaviour and using raw materials	53

Physical processes

Electricity and magnetism	71
Forces and motion	76
Waves	81
The Earth and beyond	86
Energy resources and energy transfer	89
Radioactivity	92
Index	inside back cover

Introduction

This book has been specifically designed to help you prepare for your GCSE exams in the easiest and most effective way. Keep this book with you throughout your revision – it is the key to your success.

How to use this book

All the information you need to know for your course is presented as a series of brief facts and explanations. these will help you understand and remember your work. You can work through the book chapter by chapter or you can find individual topics by using the index at the back of the book. The example below shows how pages are organised to help you revise each topic.

Running header shows you the section this topic comes into.

Examiner's tips show you how to get extra marks or avoid common mistakes.

Topic header.

Use this space to write your own notes. They will help you remember better.

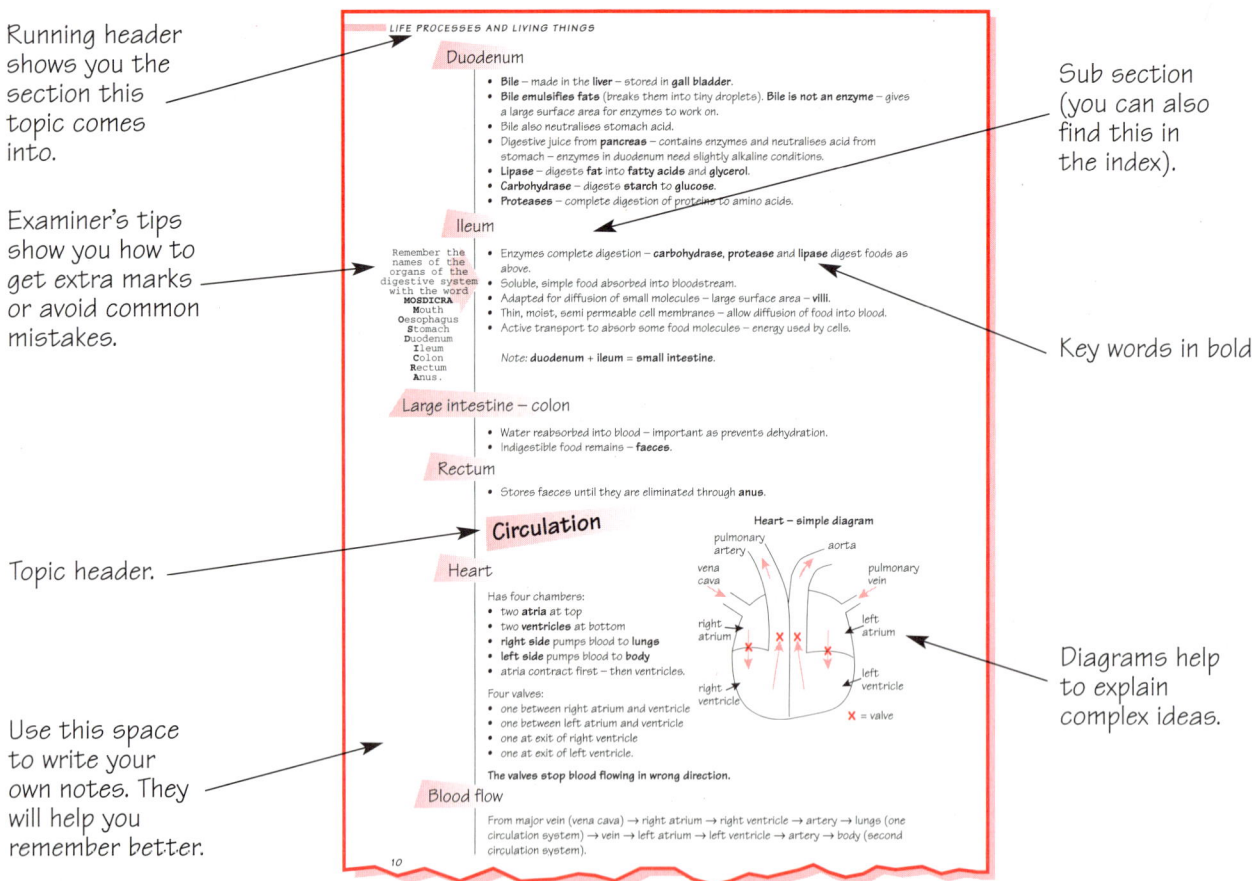

Sub section (you can also find this in the index).

Key words in bold.

Diagrams help to explain complex ideas.

Preparing your revision programme

In most subjects you will have coursework, homework, revision, practice examination questions and a final examination. The examination may cause you the most anxiety. With proper preparation, however, you do not need to worry. Remember that there is a short test at the end of each topic. This test will help your understanding and boost your memory. Make sure that you have allowed enough time to revise your work and make a list of all the things you have to do and your coursework deadlines.

The examiner's report

Every year the examiners publish reports on the previous year's examinations. The reports show areas in the examinations where students have performed well or badly and also highlight the areas where students lost marks.

- If answers are given to questions you must select from these. You cannot make up your own.
- With questions where alternative answers are provided, don't assume you have to use every answer once only.
- Draw graphs carefully. Use a pencil and ruler. Marks are awarded for accuracy. And remember, lines of best fit do not have to be straight lines – they can be curved!
- Do not write alternative answers. Writing two answers when only one is needed will mean no marks if one of the answers is wrong.
- Candidates often lose marks on the easier questions. Be careful with all of your answers.
- Take care not to rush answers in case you make a simple mistake.
- Look at the marks for the question – that is roughly how many different points you should make.

Common areas of difficulty

Biology

- Learn definition of osmosis. page 22
- Learn how fossils are formed. Remember evolution takes millions of years. page 28
- Size is a reason for diffusion occurring or not occurring. page 22
- Learn the respiration equation. Be able to distinguish between respiration and breathing. page 12
- The Sun is never a good answer to anything in biology, the answer will be light or heat. pages 18–19
- DNA and protein synthesis is difficult. page 26

Chemistry

- Properties of metals are important when explaining why materials are used for certain functions. page 48
- Learn what is meant by neutralisation. page 51
- Learn about simple chemical word equations and how to balance simple equations. page 43
- Know the difference between electrons and ions. page 39
- Learn bonding carefully, know about the ionic structure of metals and some common compounds. page 39

Physics

- Remember to use units after calculation answers. page 75
- Learn optical devices and know the difference between real and virtual. page 81
- If you are not that interested in astronomy you must learn it thoroughly. page 86
- Do not confuse current, potential difference, resistance, charge etc. page 71
- Carefully learn diffraction and refraction diagrams. page 82
- Always write the equation down before you calculate the answer. page 85

Life processes and living things

Life processes and cell activity

Characteristics of living things

Biology – **science of living things.**

- **Zoology** – study of **animals**.
- **Botany** – study of **plants**.
- **Microbiology** – study of **bacteria**, **viruses**, and **fungi**.
  To be considered as living, all of the following **seven characteristics must be present**. Some non-living things have some of these characteristics but never all seven, e.g. a car can move, respire and feed (use oxygen to burn fuel) but it is *not* alive!
- **Movement** – living things can move – animals their whole bodies – plants parts of their bodies, e.g. leaves turn towards the Sun, flowers can open and close.
- **Respiration** – **release of energy from food** – essential to all life – provides energy to carry out living functions – most organisms use oxygen to respire.
- **Sensitivity** – living things detect and respond to changes in the environment – animals respond quickly by moving – plants usually respond slowly by growing.
- **Feeding** – all living things need food – provides **energy** through respiration and other essential substances, e.g. proteins, minerals etc.
- **Excretion** – removal from body of waste products, e.g. urea, carbon dioxide, water, from chemical reactions inside cells. *Note:* It is *not* removal of waste from digestion – this is called **egestion** or **elimination**.
- **Reproduction** – all living things produce young – plants and animals reproduce so that species continues after they die.
- **Growth** – all living things increase in size – animals grow until adult – some plants never stop growing.

> Remember these by the phrase
> **MRS FERG**
> **m**ovement
> **r**espiration
> **s**ensitivity
> **f**eeding
> **e**xcretion
> **r**eproduction
> **g**rowth.

Cells

All living things are made up of cells.
Each living thing *may be* made up of millions of cells or just one cell, e.g. simple animal called Amoeba.

Animal cells

All animal cells have three basic parts:
- **cell membrane** – outside wall of cell – allows certain chemicals to move in and out of cell
- **cytoplasm** – contains many tiny structures which keep cell alive
- **nucleus** – control centre of cell – contains chemical information needed to make living thing.
  Note: Human red blood cells do *not* have nuclei – more space to carry oxygen.

> It is very important to learn the names of the parts of plant and animal cells.

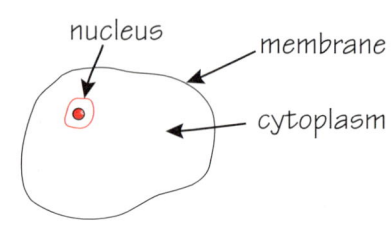

animal cell

LIFE PROCESSES AND CELL ACTIVITY

Plant cells contain all **features of animal cells**, but can have **some extra ones**.

Plant cells

Test yourself! Can you draw and label the cells without looking? This is important!

- **Cellulose Cell Wall** – gives plant cell strength – makes it tough and rigid.
- **Vacuole** – a space filled with water – when full of water the plant cell is strong and rigid – said to be **turgid**.
- **chloroplasts** – contains green **chlorophyll** – absorbs light which plant uses to make food to grow.

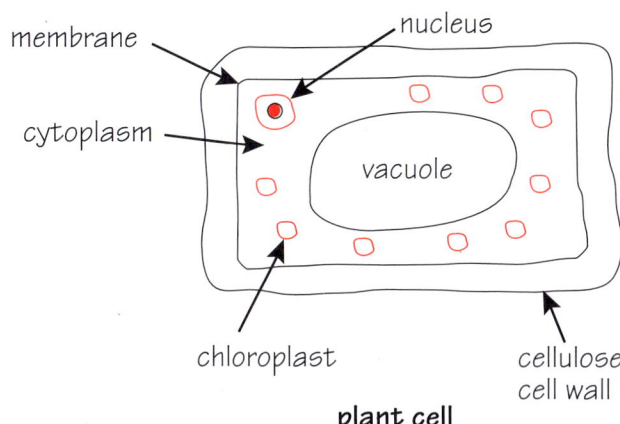

plant cell

Cells, tissues, organs and systems

Most living things have many different parts, e.g. animals have muscle, blood – plants have seeds, leaves.
The cells of these different parts have features that make them specialised to do certain jobs.

Cells can form:
- **tissues** – specialised groups of identical cells – have **same job**
- **organ** – many tissues grouped together – have **same job**
- **system** – a lot of organs grouped together – have **same job**
- **organism** – a lot of systems grouped together.

Examples

Try to learn the names of some cells, organs, and systems.

- **Muscle tissue** – contains lots of identical muscle cells.
  Lung – organ containing different tissues – muscle + blood + nerve + other tissues.
  Respiratory system – containing different organs – lung + trachea + diaphragm + ribs and muscles.
- **Glandular tissue** – a collection of glandular cells (producing enzymes etc.).
  Stomach – organ containing different tissues – glandular + nerve + muscle + blood + other tissues.
  Digestive system – includes different organs – mouth + oesophagus + stomach + intestines + other organs.
- **Xylem tissue** – lots of xylem cells (transport water in plants).
  Leaf – an organ which contains different tissues – xylem + phloem + mesophyll + epidermis.

7

LIFE PROCESSES AND LIVING THINGS

Life processes and cell activity
Questions

1. What is the study of plants called? _____
2. What is the study of animals called? _____
3. What is responding to changes in the environment called? _____
4. What is the release of energy from food called? _____
5. What is removing waste products from the body called? _____
6. What is removing the waste from digestion called? _____
7. What is producing new members of the species called? _____
8. What is increasing in size called? _____
9. Which gas is commonly used in respiration? _____
10. Which characteristic of living things is responsible for producing energy? _____
11. Name the seven characteristics of living things.
    _____
    _____
    _____
    _____
    _____
    _____
    _____
12. Which phrase helps you to remember these characteristics? _____
13. What are the inside contents of a cell called? _____
14. Which part of a cell controls its functions? _____
15. What is the outside of a plant cell called? _____
16. In which part of a plant cell is chlorophyll found? _____
17. Which part of a plant cell is filled with water? _____
18. What is a group of cells with the same function called? _____
19. What is a group of tissues with one function called? _____
20. What is a group of organs working for one function called? _____
21. What do a group of organ systems make up? _____
22. What features of plant cells do animal cells not have? _____
23. What is a neurone an example of? _____
24. What is the heart an example of? _____
25. What is the stomach an example of? _____

Humans as organisms

Nutrition

Humans need seven types of food in their diet:
- **carbohydrate** – e.g. **starch, glucose, sugar, glycogen** – used to make **energy**
- **protein** – made from **amino acids** – used for growth and repair of cells – enzymes and some hormones are proteins
- **fat** – made from **fatty acids** and **glycerol** – used to make energy – part of cell membranes
- **minerals** – like **iron** – red blood cells – **lack of** = **anaemia**, and **calcium** in bones and teeth
- **vitamins** like C – lack of = **scurvy**, and lack of D in bones and teeth = **rickets**
- **water** – solvent for many chemicals in body
- **fibre** – roughage – helps food travel along digestive system.

Digestion

- Carbohydrate, protein and fat are insoluble.
- **Digestion breaks down large, insoluble, complex molecules into smaller, simpler, soluble molecules.**
- **Enzymes carry out digestion – speed up chemical changes – catalysts.**

Digestive system

Test yourself – copy the diagram then label it from memory.

Mouth

- Chewing begins to break up food – easier to swallow.
- **Saliva** lubricates food – easier to swallow.
- Saliva contains enzyme – **carbohydrase** – starts digestion of starch to glucose.

Oesophagus

- Gullet – food squeezed by muscles – **peristalsis** – how food moves inside the gut.
- Produces no enzymes.

Stomach

- **Hydrochloric acid** kills germs and creates best conditions for enzymes.
- **Enzyme gastric protease** – digests protein to amino acids.

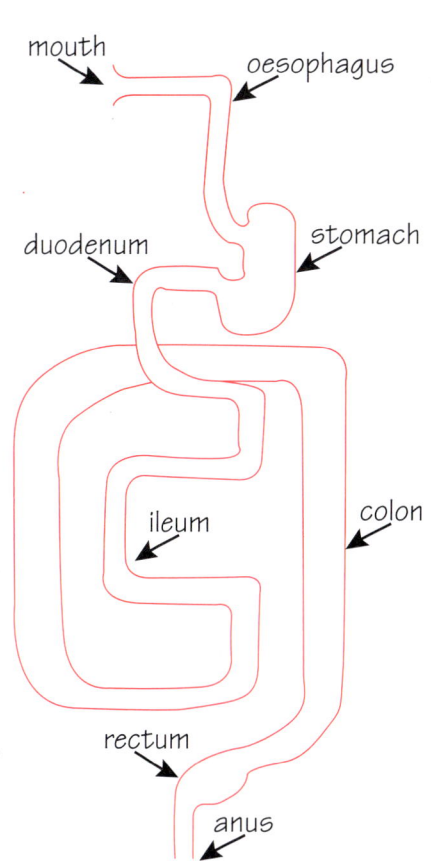

9

LIFE PROCESSES AND LIVING THINGS

Duodenum

- **Bile** – made in the **liver** – stored in **gall bladder**.
- **Bile emulsifies fats** (breaks them into tiny droplets). **Bile is not an enzyme** – gives a large surface area for enzymes to work on.
- Bile also neutralises stomach acid.
- Digestive juice from **pancreas** – contains enzymes and neutralises acid from stomach – enzymes in duodenum need slightly alkaline conditions.
- **Lipase** – digests **fat** into **fatty acids** and **glycerol**.
- **Carbohydrase** – digests **starch** to **glucose**.
- **Proteases** – complete digestion of proteins to amino acids.

Ileum

Remember the names of the organs of the digestive system with the word **MOSDICRA**
Mouth
Oesophagus
Stomach
Duodenum
Ileum
Colon
Rectum
Anus.

- Enzymes complete digestion – **carbohydrase**, **protease** and **lipase** digest foods as above.
- Soluble, simple food absorbed into bloodstream.
- Adapted for diffusion of small molecules – large surface area – **villi**.
- Thin, moist, semi permeable cell membranes – allow diffusion of food into blood.
- Active transport to absorb some food molecules – energy used by cells.

Note: **duodenum + ileum = small intestine**.

Large intestine – colon

- Water reabsorbed into blood – important as prevents dehydration.
- Indigestible food remains – **faeces**.

Rectum

- Stores faeces until they are eliminated through **anus**.

Circulation

Heart

Has four chambers:
- two **atria** at top
- two **ventricles** at bottom
- **right side** pumps blood to **lungs**
- **left side** pumps blood to **body**
- atria contract first – then ventricles.

Four valves:
- one between right atrium and ventricle
- one between left atrium and ventricle
- one at exit of right ventricle
- one at exit of left ventricle.

The valves stop blood flowing in wrong direction.

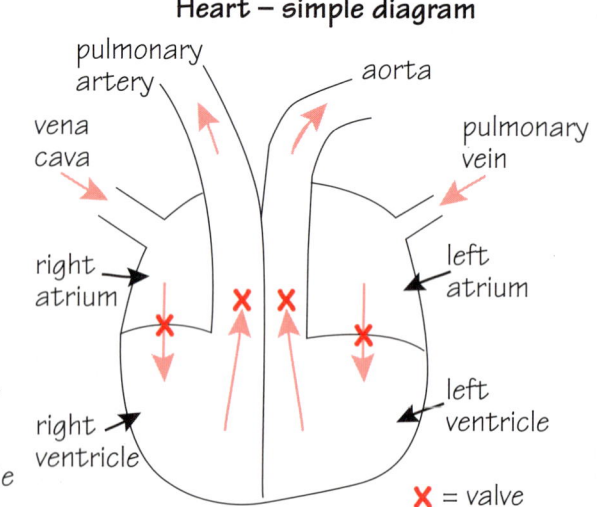

Heart – simple diagram

Blood flow

From major vein (vena cava) → right atrium → right ventricle → artery → lungs (one circulation system) → vein → left atrium → left ventricle → artery → body (second circulation system).

HUMANS AS ORGANISMS

Blood vessels

Arteries
- Thick walls – elastic – have muscle.
- Need to withstand high pressure.
- Carry blood **away** from the heart.
- Deep in the body for protection.

Remember A = Artery = Away.

Veins
- Thinner walls than arteries.
- Have **valves** to keep blood flowing towards heart.
- Near muscles to help squeeze blood back to heart.

Vein = in.

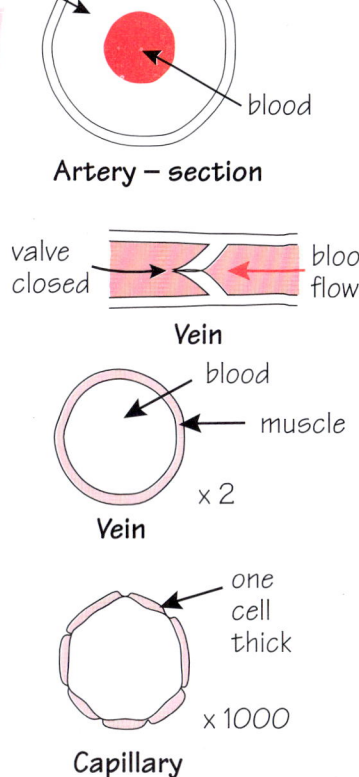

Capillaries
- Very thin – walls one cell thick.
- Exchange food, oxygen, carbon dioxide, waste, cell products, between blood and organs.
- Capillary exchange mechanisms in all organs, e.g. ileum – villi, lung – alveoli, kidney – nephron.
- Provide very large surface area for diffusion.

Blood

Contains **red cells**, **white cells**, **platelets** and **plasma**.

Red Cells
- Carry **oxygen** in **haemoglobin**.
- Oxygen + haemoglobin → Oxyhaemoglobin – in lungs.
- Oxyhaemoglobin → Oxygen + haemoglobin – in capillaries near body cells – oxygen into cells for respiration.
- No nucleus – more room to carry oxygen.
- Made in bone marrow – live approximately 120 days.
- Poisoned by **carbon monoxide** – person suffocates from lack of oxygen.

White cells
- Have nuclei.
- Made in bone marrow.
- **Immunity** – defend the body against invaders – microbes, e.g. bacteria, viruses.
- Detect invaders and ingest (eat) them.
- **Antibodies** – made by white cells – destroy microbes and foreign tissue.
- **Antitoxins** – destroy poisons produced by microbes.
- **Immune system memory** – once you have had a disease you are immune – **vaccinations** trigger immune memory – **boosters** needed as a reminder for some diseases.

Note: you get lots of colds because the virus is different each time.

Antibodies do not stay in blood forever – your immune system remembers how to make them when needed.

Platelets
- Made in bone marrow – from parts of much larger cells.
- React to cell damage / air.
- Produce fibres to trap red blood cells and **clot the blood**.

Plasma
- Liquid part of blood.
- Dissolves **carbon dioxide** – carries it to lungs.
- Carries dissolved **food from small intestine to liver** and all cells.
- Carries all cells.
- Carries **urea from liver to kidneys**.

11

LIFE PROCESSES AND LIVING THINGS

Respiration

Lungs – special cells – ciliated epithelium – have cilia – clean lungs.

Breathing in
- Ribs move up and out – by muscles contracting.
- **Diaphragm** muscles contract – diaphragm moves down – flattens.
- Volume of chest increases.
- Pressure decreases (Boyle's law – physics).
- Air pressure forces air into lungs.

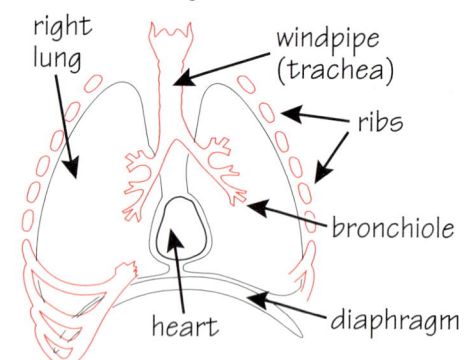

System includes: **trachea, bronchi, bronchioles, alveoli**.

Alveoli
- Air sacs – provide a large surface area for gas exchange.
- Thin – about 2 cells between air in air sac and blood.
- Moist – lined with mucus – oxygen dissolves in mucus.
- Selectively permeable membranes – allow diffusion of gases.
- Good blood supply – capillaries cover alveoli – gases **oxygen** and **carbon dioxide** exchanged.

Internal respiration – production of energy within cells.

> In exams remember to say – in lungs O_2 is picked up by blood – CO_2 is released by blood.

Aerobic respiration

> glucose + oxygen → carbon dioxide + water + energy

- Glucose carried in plasma.
- Oxygen carried in red blood cells.
- Cell cytoplasm – **mitochondria** – contains enzymes for respiration.
- Carbon dioxide carried away by plasma.
- Water – **metabolic water** – important source of water in desert animals.

Energy use
- Making molecules, e.g. proteins from amino acids.
- Muscle contraction.
- Heat production in birds and mammals – constant body temperature – homeostasis (see below).
- **Active Transport** – diffusion of small molecules against a diffusion gradient, e.g. glucose in the kidney nephron, minerals in plant roots.

Exercise
- Muscles respire **aerobically** for a short time – they rapidly run out of oxygen – **anaerobic** respiration starts.
- Glucose broken into two molecules of **lactic acid** – energy released so muscles can continue to work.
- **Lactic acid** builds up as anaerobic respiration continues.
- **Oxygen debt** results – oxygen needed to remove all lactic acid after exercise.
- Anaerobic produces much **less** energy than aerobic.
- **Carbon dioxide** is **not** produced by anaerobic respiration.

> Heavy exercise – still breathing – oxygen still entering muscles – aerobic respiration happens when enough oxygen present – carbon dioxide produced. Anaerobic respiration when not enough oxygen – lactic acid produced. Aerobic and anaerobic respiration can happen at same time.

Nervous system

Central nervous system (CNS)

- Brain.
- Spinal cord.

Neurons

- Sensory – messages from receptors to CNS.
- Motor – messages from CNS to effectors, i.e. muscles, glands and organs.
- Relay – mostly in CNS – messages between sensory and motor neurons.

Learn this.

Stimulus → receptor → co-ordinator → effector → response

Eye

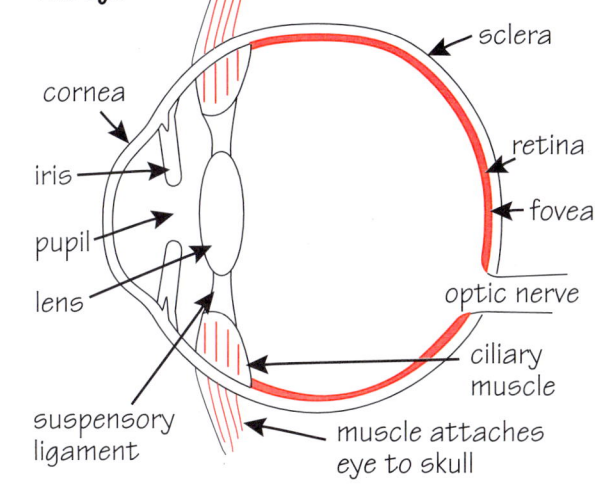

The eye

- **Cornea** – transparent.
- **Sclera** – tough – protection.
- **Iris** – muscles control size of **pupil** – large in dim light – small in bright light.
- **Pupil** – hole for light to enter eye.
- **Retina** – light sensitive cells.
- **Lens** – shape controlled by **suspensory ligaments** and **ciliary muscle**.
- **Optic nerve** – takes nerve impulses from retina to brain.
- **Fovea** – depression towards centre of retina where vision most acute.

Image detection

Light enters eye → cornea and lens focus light on retina → receptor cells send message via optic nerve to brain → brain interprets image.

Focusing images

- Distant object – ciliary muscle relaxed – lens thin.
- Near object – ciliary muscle contracts – lens thick.

Reflex action, e.g. knee-jerk reflex

Important – you must be able to analyse any given situation in terms of stimulus → receptor → co-ordinator → effector → response.

- **Receptor** detects **stimulus**, e.g. tap on knee.
- Sends message (**impulse**) – sensory nerve to CNS – **co-ordinator**, in this case = spinal cord.
- **Synapse** – gap between sensory neuron and relay neuron – chemical messenger crosses gap – **neurotransmitter** – passes impulse to relay neuron.
- **Synapse** – gap between relay and motor neuron – neurotransmitter – passes impulse to motor neuron.
- Motor neuron carries impulse to **effector**, in this case = thigh muscle.
- Effector produces **response**, in this case = leg moves forward.

Effectors make muscles move or glands secrete, e.g. saliva at the smell of food.

LIFE PROCESSES AND LIVING THINGS

Hormones

Control and co-ordinate many body processes.

Blood sugar

Monitored and controlled by pancreas.

Glucose level in blood too high
- Pancreas releases **hormone insulin** into blood.
- **Insulin** picked up by **liver** from blood.
- Liver cells take glucose from blood – convert it to **glycogen** – stored.
- Blood sugar returns to normal.

Learn insulin/glucagon – often confused in exams.

Glucose level in blood too low
- **Pancreas** releases hormone **glucagon** into blood.
- **Glucagon** picked up by **liver** from blood.
- **Liver cells** convert **glycogen** to glucose – glucose released into blood.
- Blood sugar returns to normal.

Menstrual cycle

Draw a diagram like this to help you remember blood sugar control.

Controlled by hormones from the **pituitary gland** in the brain and the **ovaries**.
- Day 1–5 – **period** occurs.
- Days 6–13 – **uterus** lining thickens caused by **oestrogen** and **progesterone** from ovary, prepares to receive fertilised ovum – ovum maturing, caused by hormone **FSH** from pituitary.
- Day 14 – ovulation – caused by hormone **LH** from pituitary.
- Day 15–28 – embryo implants. Or not pregnant – uterus lining stops developing – lack of hormones.
- Day 29 = day 1 – uterus lining shed if not pregnant – period.

Menstrual cycle diagram: pituitary → LH / FSH → ovary → ovum matures → ovulation → oestrogen → stops FSH release.

Fertility treatment
FSH given – stimulates ovum development in ovaries – more than one may mature – multiple births.

Contraception
Oestrogen given – inhibits FSH production by pituitary – no eggs mature – none released.
Problem – body thinks it's pregnant – side effects – possible weight gain, sickness, long-term effects.
Take with medical supervision only.

Water balance

Hormone – **anti-diuretic hormone** – ADH – produced by **pituitary gland**. See **Homeostasis**.

HUMANS AS ORGANISMS

Homeostasis

Control of the body's internal environment to keep it constant.

Lungs
- Remove carbon dioxide – waste product of respiration.
- Some water lost as breath is moist.

Liver
- Excess **amino acids** broken down into **urea** + carbohydrate.
- Carbohydrate – energy source – stored as **glycogen** or used in respiration.
- **Urea** enters blood and removed by **kidneys**.

Kidneys

Read your own teacher's notes about kidney machines – Dialysis.

- Filter the blood via kidney nephron.
- All small substances removed, e.g. water, urea, salt and glucose.
- Glucose needed by body – all glucose reabsorbed by nephron by **active transport** – cells use energy to do this.
- Some salt – sodium and chloride ions – reabsorbed.
- Water – see **Osmoregulation** below.
- Urea, salt ions and water are excreted – **urine** – stored in the **bladder** – eliminated as necessary.

Osmoregulation – water regulation – most important job of kidney

Brain monitors blood concentration.

Learn this by drawing your own flow diagram!

Blood is too concentrated – not enough water
- Feeling of thirst – drink water.
- **Pituitary** produces **ADH** – travels in blood to kidney.
- Makes **kidney nephron more permeable** – reabsorbs water back into blood.
- **Urine is more concentrated** – less water lost.
- Blood returns to normal.

Blood too dilute – too much water
- **Pituitary** releases less **ADH**.
- **Urine more dilute** – more water lost.
- Kidney nephron is less permeable to water.
- Blood returns to normal.

Skin
- Sweating – loses heat, water, salt ions and some urea; temperature control.

Temperature control

Thermoregulatory centre in brain monitors core body temperature.

Environment too hot
- Skin temperature **receptor** – causes impulse in sensory nerve → brain (co-ordinator).
- Brain sends messages – nerve impulse and hormone – to blood vessels in skin – dilate (get wider) – more blood to skin surface – more heat lost.
- Also message to sweat glands – sweat on skin – liquid evaporates – cool down.
  Note: capillary muscles = **effector**
         dilating = **response**.

Environment too cold
- Brain and skin detect.
- Message to skin blood vessels to constrict – less blood to skin – less heat lost.
- Brain – message to muscles to shiver – produces heat by respiration.

LIFE PROCESSES AND LIVING THINGS

Diseases

- Caused by **microbes** that invade body.
- Caused by toxins – poisons – produced by growing microbes.
- Growth of microbes in cells cause cell death.
- Made much worse by person being weak, e.g. in the disease AIDS.
- Usually need a lot of microbes to cause disease – unhygienic conditions, e.g. food poisoning (bacteria) – or contact with infection, e.g. chickenpox (virus).

Microbes

- Bacteria – much smaller than animal cells – contain cytoplasm, membrane and cell wall – genes in cytoplasm, *not* in a nucleus – most bacteria are harmless and very useful, e.g. grow in soil → nitrogen cycle – only a few cause disease.
- Antibiotics stop bacteria growing – penicillin stops cell wall production – bacteria burst and die.
- **Viruses** – much smaller than bacteria – contain protein and a few genes – can only grow inside living cells – take over cell functions – cell bursts open and dies when viruses reproduce.

Defence

- **Skin** – barrier to microbes.
- **Blood clot** – wounds quickly sealed – prevents entry of microbes.
- **Mucus** – sticky to trap microorganisms – protects nose, mouth, then lungs and stomach – open to outside.
- **Stomach** has acid – kills most microbes.
- **Immune system** – white blood cells – antibodies – see blood, circulation.

Drugs

These are any chemicals that enter the body and have an effect.
They can be:
- **useful** – e.g. paracetamol – pain relief, antibiotics – kill microbes
- **harmful** – e.g. nicotine – dependence on cigarettes, alcohol – liver problems
- **very dangerous** – e.g. paracetamol – can be fatal with overdose, heroin – addictive, cocaine – addictive – withdrawal problems – very hard to quit.

Drug misuse

- Effect of drugs on a person depends upon person's state of health and mind.
- Same drug can affect two different people in very different ways.

Solvents

- Seriously affect behaviour, drug is in control.
- Damage to liver, lungs and brain.
- Most deaths caused by inhaling vomit when unconscious.

Tobacco

- Nicotine is addictive – affects blood pressure – calms people down – hard to give up.
- Other chemicals in cigarettes cause cancer – throat, lung, stomach.
- Breathing problems – emphysema, bronchitis.
- Carbon monoxide, in smoke – blood carries less oxygen – high blood pressure.
- Heart and blood vessels affected – heart disease, artery disease.

Alcohol

- Affects nervous system – small amounts – mild anaesthetic – slows reactions, larger amounts – affects motor control – movement, speech – person is not in control – coma – unconsciousness can follow – can be fatal.
- Heavy drinking for a long time causes severe liver damage – cirrhosis and sclerosis (hardening of tissue) – death will result – brain damage also.

Humans as organisms

Questions

1. Which three foods need digesting? _____
2. How does food travel along the digestive system? _____
3. What are the two functions of the acid in the stomach? _____
4. What is the function of bile? _____
5. What is the function of a protease? _____
6. Which chamber of the heart pumps blood to the lungs? _____
7. Which chamber of the heart pumps blood around the body? _____
8. Why do arteries have thick muscular walls? _____
9. Why do veins have valves? _____
10. What is the function of red blood cells? _____
11. Name three things carried by blood plasma. _____
12. Where in the lungs does diffusion take place? _____
13. Which type of respiration uses oxygen? _____
14. Which type of respiration does not use oxygen? _____
15. What is the order of events in any nervous response? _____
16. Which organs make up the CNS? _____
17. Which hormone reduces blood sugar level? _____
18. Which hormone raises blood sugar level? _____
19. Which hormone causes ova to mature? _____
20. Which hormone causes ovulation? _____
21. What happens to excess amino acids in the body? _____
22. What effect does ADH have on the kidney nephron? _____
23. What is the difference between bacteria and viruses? _____
24. What causes people to be addicted to cigarettes? _____

LIFE PROCESSES AND LIVING THINGS

Green plants as organisms
Photosynthesis

- Plants **make food** by **photosynthesis**.

> You must learn this equation.

$$\text{carbon dioxide} + \text{water} \xrightarrow[\text{chlorophyll}]{\text{light}} \text{glucose} + \text{oxygen}$$

- Photosynthesis controlled by **enzymes**.
- All **enzyme reaction rates are variable** depending on the conditions.

Carbon dioxide

> Look up the experiments on photosynthesis! **Remember:** you test leaves for starch using iodine, you need meths to remove the green colour from the leaf first!

- **Increased carbon dioxide – increased photosynthesis** – only up to the point where enzymes are working as fast as they can.
- Increase in carbon dioxide after this has little effect.
- Limited light will stop an increase in carbon dioxide from having any effect.

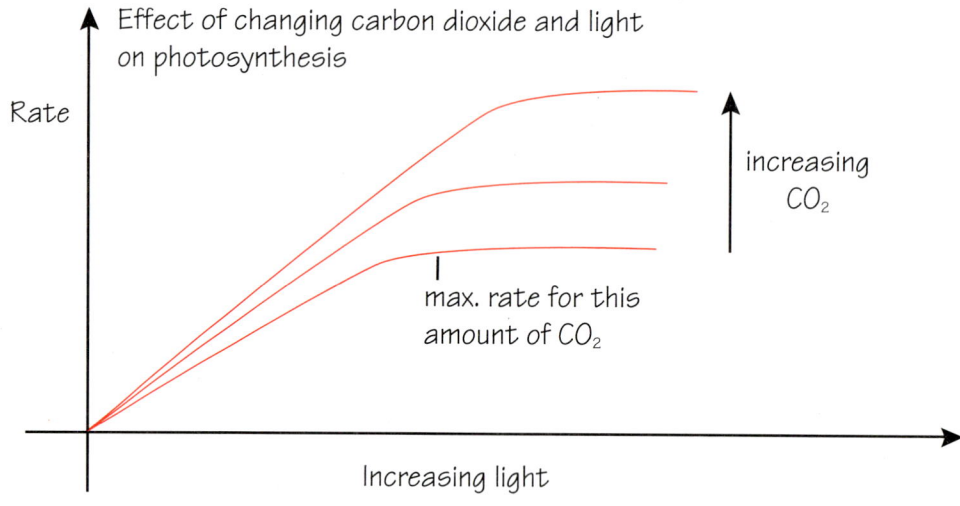

> When drawing graphs
> - **Use a pencil**.
> - Mark your points clearly with an X.
> - Draw a line of best fit.
> - Use as much of the graph paper as possible – use the largest scale you can.

Light

- **Increased light – increased photosynthesis** – until enzymes are working as fast as they can.
- Increasing light after this has little effect.
- Carbon dioxide limited – will stop increase in light from having any effect.
- Low temperature stops increase in light from having any effect.
- Light absorbed by **chlorophyll** in **chloroplast**.
- Not all plant cells have chloroplasts – e.g. **epidermal** cells have a different function – protect plant.
- Specialised cells in leaf called **palisade mesophyll** – specially adapted for photosynthesis – elongated shape to absorb light – more chloroplasts.

18

Temperature

- **Increased temperature** – **rate of photosynthesis increases** up to the **optimum temperature** for the enzyme.
- **Optimum temperature** – enzyme shape is a perfect fit (lock and key idea).
- Above this temperature enzyme shape starts to change – no longer fits perfectly – rate of reaction decreases – enzyme **denatures** at **high temperature**.
- Optimum temperature for photosynthesis different depending on environment plant is adapted to, e.g. desert plants adapted to higher temperatures than British plants.

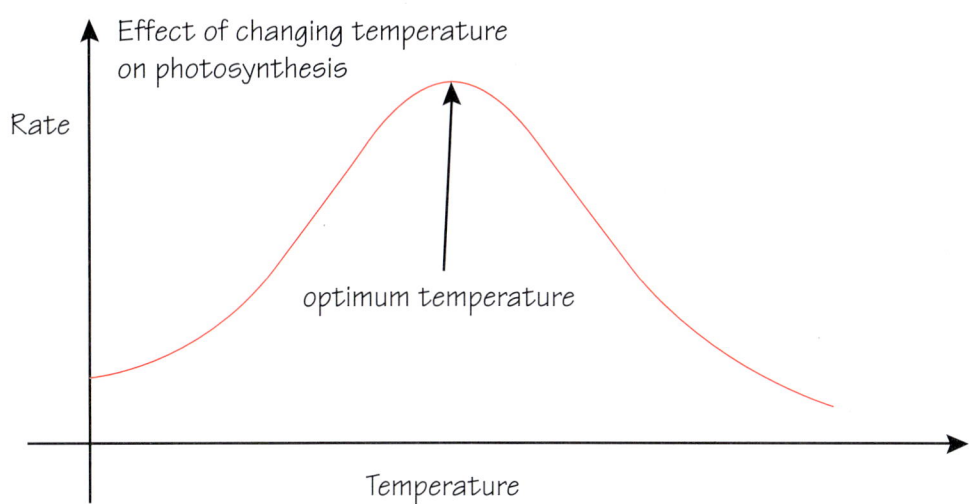

Effect of changing temperature on photosynthesis

Photosynthesis and assimilation

Assimilation means **how food is used.**

In plants the sugars produced by photosynthesis are:
- used to produce **starch** – stored as a future energy/raw material store
- converted to **cellulose** to make cell walls
- with **addition of nitrogen** and sometimes **phosphorus** and **sulphur** – converted into protein.

Also:
- **proteins** are used for **growth**
- **glucose** is used to **produce energy** needed for growth.

Plants store carbohydrate as starch and **not sugars like glucose**.
This is because:
- starch is **insoluble**
- glucose causes large amounts of water to enter cells by osmosis – starch does not
- osmosis – see later section.

LIFE PROCESSES AND LIVING THINGS

Transport of nutrients

Glucose and other nutrients are transported by **phloem** cells – from leaves to:
- storage organs, e.g. roots
- growing regions, e.g. shoot tips.
* To make essential chemicals of life plants must absorb minerals through roots.
* Different minerals have different functions in plant.

Minerals and plant health

Nitrates
* **Essential** for the **synthesis of protein**.
* Remember **glucose** contains the elements carbon, hydrogen and oxygen.
* **Proteins** contain these together with **nitrogen**.
* Protein is needed to make **membranes, DNA, enzymes** and **chlorophyll**.

Nitrate deficiency
* Causes poor growth and yellowing of leaves.
* Little protein made – no new cells as no cell membranes made, no enzymes to control cells and no chlorophyll.
* Plants try to **compensate** – produce new leaves – have to move any nitrogen they have to the growth areas – older leaves become yellow and die off.

Summary: **Plants** that are **stunted in growth** with **yellow older leaves** are **nitrate** or **nitrogen deficient**.

Potassium
* Needed for **synthesis** of **some enzymes**.
* Photosynthesis and respiration impaired – plant will have many problems.
* Cannot synthesise chemicals and produce energy.

Potassium deficiency
* Growth limited – not as badly affected as nitrate deficiency.
* Young leaves are yellow as **chlorophyll** synthesis restricted – enzyme problems.
* Leaves eventually turn green as plant moves resources to compensate – areas of cell death due to lack of enzymes.

Summary: **Potassium deficiency** causes **yellow leaves with dead spots**.

Phosphate
* Needed to **synthesise some proteins** but not all.
* If essential proteins cannot be made growth will be affected.
* Phosphate has an **important role** in **photosynthesis** and **respiration**.

Phosphate deficiency
* Root growth severely affected – roots short with few side roots.
* Young leaves produced that are purple in colour.
* Chlorophyll not synthesised properly – enzyme problems.

Summary: **Phosphate deficiency** causes **stunted root growth** and **purple younger leaves**.

Plant hormones

- **Hormones** – **control plant growth**.

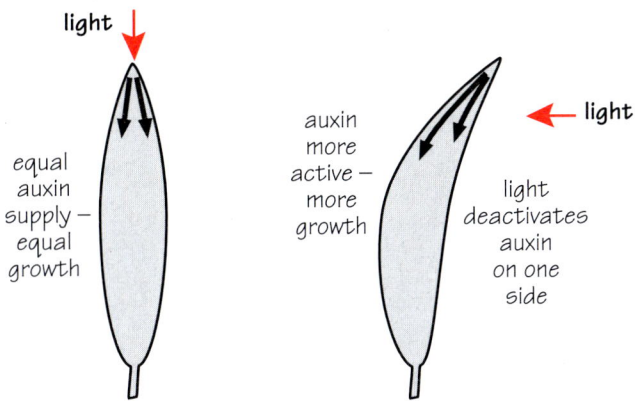

- **Shoots** grow towards light – phototropism – away from gravity – negative geotropism.
- **Roots** grow towards water and gravity – away from light.
- Shoots bend towards light because of hormone – **auxin** – causes lengthening of cells.
- Shoot tip produces auxin – this moves back down plant stem.
- Light **deactivates auxin**.
- If light from one side only – more auxin on shade side – this side lengthens more – shoot bends over **towards the light**.

Roots

- Rooting powders – used to promote growth of stem cuttings.
- Hormone promotes the growth of healthy roots on the cut stem.
- Many plants produced very quickly by promoting root growth on many stem cuttings.

Fruit

- Hormones sprayed on flowers – causes formation of fruit – fruit has not been fertilised and is seedless.
- Fruit also bigger than normal – energy has not been used to produce seeds.
- Hormones also sprayed to speed up or slow down fruit development – on the tree or after fruit picked – farmer able to produce crop at best time for climate and market.

Weedkillers

- Growth hormones sprayed onto plants – grow too quickly – run short of energy and die.
- The hormones are selective for certain types of plant – weedkiller works from within – when the plant dies the hormone should be broken down in the soil.

Benefits

You may need to discuss this in the form of a short essay!

- Production of many new plants by cuttings – identical to the parent plant.
- Development of seedless fruit.
- Selective weedkillers that do not pollute the soil.

Problems

- What if the plant hormones aren't broken down in the soil? Can enter food chain – could cause problems for other plants and animals.

LIFE PROCESSES AND LIVING THINGS

Transport and water relations – transpiration

Copy diagram and label cells from memory.

- Plants absorb most water through **root hair cells** – adapted to increase surface area for absorption.
- Plants lose water through leaves – dependent on the structure of the leaves.
- Water evaporates from spongy mesophyll cells → enters the spaces in leaf → diffuses towards the stomata pore → evaporates from the leaf.
- Water that is lost from the leaves is replaced by water from roots.
- **Water flows from roots through stem and to leaves in xylem vessels.**
- Movement of water called **transpiration stream** – fastest on hot, windy, dry, sunny days – slower on cold, wet and dark days.

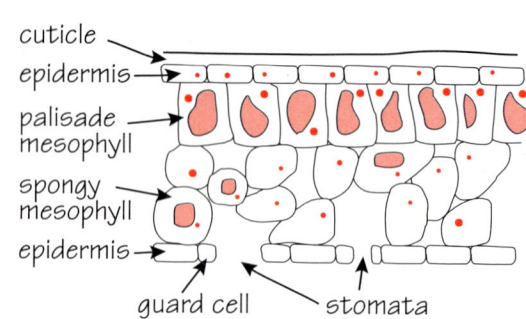

Water regulations

- **Stomata** – holes in underside of leaves – restrict the loss of water.
- **Guard cells** – special cells that open or close stomata.

Daylight/plant has a lot of water:
- photosynthesising as fast as possible
- stomata wide open to allow transpiration at maximum rate.

Plant is short of water/dark:
- stomata close – restricts water loss
- photosynthesis also slows down or stops.

Plants that live **in dry climates** are **adapted to restrict water loss by:**
- having thicker cuticle – prevents water evaporating from upper leaf surface
- reducing leaves to spikes, e.g. cacti.

Osmosis

Plant cells absorb or lose water by osmosis depending upon concentration of solutes.

Learn your teacher's definition of osmosis.

- **Gaining water** – dilute outside cell – concentrated inside – water enters cell by osmosis – cell swells.
- **Turgid** – cell full of water – turgid cells important – gives cells support.
- **Losing water** – concentrated outside cell – more dilute inside – water leaves cell by osmosis – cell shrinks.
- **Flaccid** – when only a little water is lost – plant wilts.
- **Plasmolysed** – loss of too much water – plant dies.

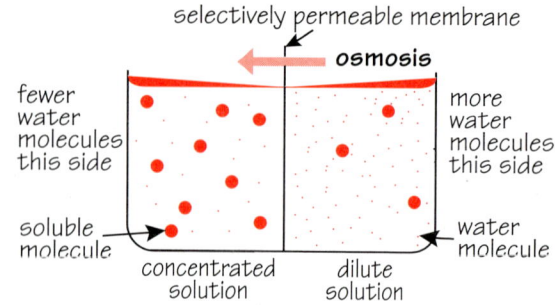

Example
Think of a plant cell as a football – the leather case is like cellulose cell wall – rubber inner tube is vacuole.
- The more air you blow into the football the harder it becomes – water entering the vacuole makes a plant cell **turgid.**
- If air is let out of the football it becomes soft – water leaving the plant vacuole makes the cell soft – **plasmolysed**.

Green plants as organisms

Questions

1. What is the green pigment in plants called and where in the cell is it found?
   _____

2. Which cells in the leaf are specially adapted for photosynthesis? _____
   _____

3. What is the name of the cells in a plant that transport water? _____

4. What is the name of the cells that transport food in a plant? _____

5. What is the name of the cells in a plant that transport minerals? _____

6. In which conditions would photosynthesis be greatest? _____

7. In which conditions would photosynthesis be worst? _____

8. In which conditions would transpiration be very high? _____

9. In which conditions would transpiration be very low? _____

10. At which time of year is photosynthesis greatest? _____

11. What is the name of the process that describes how glucose leaves and enters a plant cell? _____

12. By what process does water leave and enter a cell? _____

13. What word describes a cell full of water? _____

14. What word describes a cell that is lacking in water? _____

15. Which mineral deficiency causes very poor growth in plants? _____

16. Which mineral deficiency causes young leaves to be purple in plants? _____

17. Which mineral deficiency causes any leaves to turn yellow? _____

18. Which mineral deficiency causes dead spots on leaves? _____

19. Which mineral deficiency causes stunted root growth? _____

20. Which mineral deficiency causes the plant's older leaves to turn yellow? _____

21. How do plant shoots respond to light? _____

22. How do plant roots respond to gravity? _____

23. How do plant shoots respond to gravity? _____

LIFE PROCESSES AND LIVING THINGS

Variation, inheritance and evolution

Causes of variation

Living things of the same species are different from each other owing to two factors:

- **genes** – different living things have different genes
- **environmental** – living things live in different environment – can affect how living things grow – not enough food or nutrients – animals and plants will not grow as well – too much competition in one place – animals or plants may be stunted in development – opposite could also be true if there was very little competition.

Genetics

You must learn the names used in genetics.

- Studying how **information** is passed on from one generation to the next.
- Information is carried in **genes** which are found on **chromosomes**.
- Different genes control different **characteristics**.
- Different forms of same gene – **alleles**, e.g. brown and blue eye colour.
- **Homozygous** – individual has both alleles of a gene the same, e.g. XX, female.
- **Heterozygous** – individual has different alleles for a gene, e.g. XY, male.
- **Dominant allele** – characteristic always develops.
- **Recessive allele** – characteristic only develops when dominant allele not present.

Chromosomes

- **Genes** are found on **chromosomes**.
- Chromosomes **in pairs** in **all body cells** of **all animals** and **plants**.
- In **humans** there are **46 chromosomes** – 23 pairs in all body cells.
- **Every cell has all genes** that carry the information to make another copy of you.
- Chromosomes made from chemical called **DNA**.
- DNA has unique property that it can duplicate itself exactly.
- When cells divide they produce exact copies of chromosomes and genes.

Heredity

- Genes are passed on from one generation to next.
- Every living thing must reproduce to survive – passing genes to next generation.
- A living thing is a biological success if it leaves copies of its genes in its offspring.
- The more copies of its genes it leaves, the bigger a success it was.

Two forms of reproduction

- **Sexual** – this mixes genes – produces much more variation in living things – evolution can happen.
- **Asexual** – produces offspring that are identical – **clones** – all **genetically same**.

Cell division

Mitosis

Body cell division – repair and growth.
- Cells divide – produce copies of themselves – all pairs of chromosomes duplicated exactly.
- Two new cell nuclei receive identical sets of paired chromosomes.
- All body cells have identical chromosomes – there are occasional mistakes – **chromosome mutations**.

Meiosis

Production of sex cells
- Copies of chromosomes made in **testes of males** after puberty – in **ovaries of females** before they are born – in **ovaries** and **anthers** of **plants**.
- Pairs of chromosomes separated.
- Cell divides to form four sex cells – each cell only has one copy of the chromosome.

Human genetics

- Human cells have 46 chromosomes in nuclei.
- When ovum fertilised to produce baby, baby must also have 46 chromosomes.
- Sex cells – sperm and ova – have 23 chromosomes.
- Sperm and ovum contribute equally to embryo.
- 23 chromosomes from sperm + 23 chromosomes from ovum = 46-chromosome embryo.

Inheritance of sex

- Humans have sex chromosomes called X and Y.
- Females have two X chromosomes (XX).
- Males have one X and one Y (XY).
- When sex cells produced – sex chromosomes separate and end up in different cells.
- All ova have X chromosome only.
- Two types of sperm – one with Y chromosome – one with X chromosome.

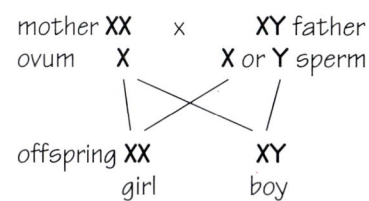

Cystic fibrosis

- Caused by **recessive gene** (c). N = normal dominant gene.
- Breathing and digestion problems – membranes do not secrete normally.
- Sufferers have a short life expectancy.
- Adults can be normal but carry a recessive cystic gene – **carrier**.
- Condition usually runs in families but may miss generations.
- Parents Nc x Nc – 25% chance of a cystic child.

Huntington's chorea

- Caused by a **dominant gene**. (H) parent Hn x nn.
- Affects the nervous system – loss of motor and sensory function – quickly leads to death.
- Person will be perfectly normal until about 35 to 45 years of age – develop Huntington's chorea – become seriously ill and die.
- By this time may have had their family and passed the gene on to children.

Sickle cell anaemia

- Caused by **recessive gene**.
- Disease is inherited from both parents who carry the gene.
- Name comes from shape of the red blood cells that disease produces.
- **Sickle cell disease** is **fatal**.
- Gene is still in populations of people who live where there is **malaria** – carriers of the gene have a greater resistance to malaria than normal people.
- So in malaria areas – NN catch malaria and die – Ns survive – ss die of sickle cell anaemia (let N = normal and s = sickle cell).

Sex-linked conditions – caused by Y chromosome in males having missing DNA.
- **Muscular dystrophy** – muscle wastage – fatal by adolescence.
- **Haemophilia** – cannot make factor 8 protein – clots the blood.
- Inherited from the mother – she carries a recessive gene on one of her X chromosomes.
- Father's X chromosome has a normal gene but Y chromosome has gene missing. E.g. haemophilia, **colour blindness**.
- Only males contract haemophilia.
- Haemophiliac males tend not to have children because of the difficulties caused by the disease.

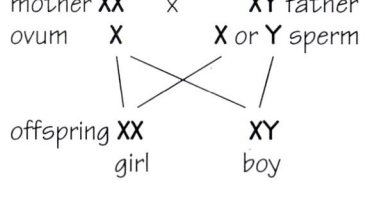

LIFE PROCESSES AND LIVING THINGS

- Only males get one form of Muscular Dystrophy – it is passed on in the same way.
- Females can be colour blind even though it is inherited in the same way – colour blind males will want to have children as the condition is not life threatening.

   Let C = normal vision and c = colour blind
   Mother (XCXc) – a carrier x father (XcY–) – colour blind
   There is a 25% chance of the genotype XcXc – a colour blind female.

Structure of DNA

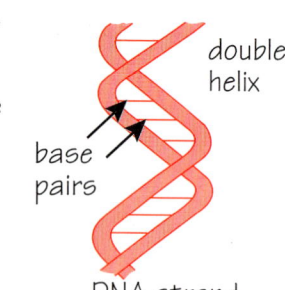

- Two long strands that coil around each other – form **double helix** shape.
- Strands linked together by **hydrogen bonds** – from one **base** to another.
- 4 bases (chemicals) in DNA – called A, T, C, and G.

DNA is able to replicate itself exactly.

- Double helix 'unzips' – each side acts as a template to build another DNA strand.
- Result is **two** double helixes of DNA.
- These separate into new cells as cell cytoplasm divides.
- Happens to **all** chromosomes (strands of DNA) at same time so the division of cells is co-ordinated.

DNA structure and protein synthesis often confused in exams - be careful.

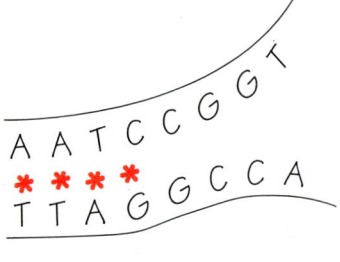

✱ = hydrogen bond

Protein synthesis

- Order of bases of DNA very important.
- Order codes for all proteins.
- Three nucleic acid bases code for one amino acid.

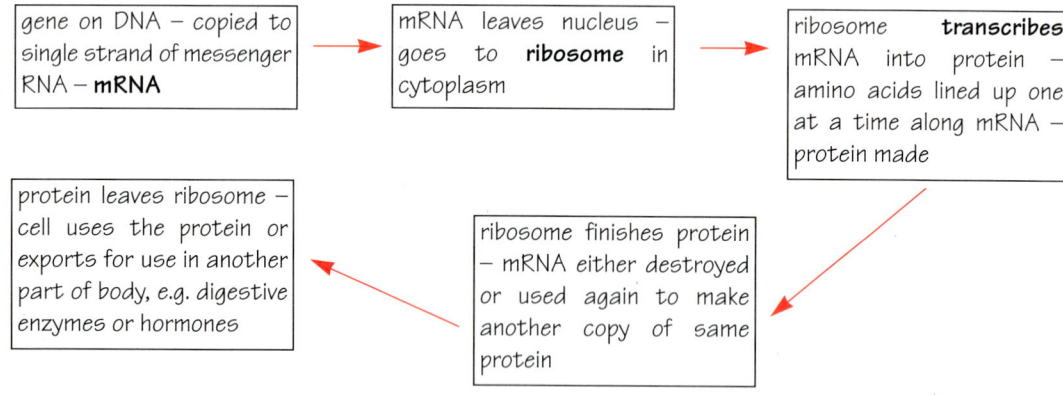

Mutation

- Change in gene code – DNA instructions changed.
- Gene mutations when ova and sperm being produced will be passed on to offspring – embryo will not survive if mutation too great – embryo usually non-viable.
- Only small mutations passed on this way, e.g. **Down's syndrome**.
- Down's syndrome – one sex cell (usually ovum) contains one extra chromosome – the embryo has 47 chromosomes instead of 46 – affects development – produces child with symptoms of Down's syndrome.

Chromosome changes in adults

- Cells divide and produce new cells – making new chromosomes can go wrong.
- **Mutations** can occur naturally with a mistake in replication of DNA.
- Dead cell is destroyed by immune system and no harm results.

VARIATION, INHERITANCE AND EVOLUTION

- Some mutations caused by **ionising radiation**, e.g. ultra violet, gamma rays, X-rays.
- Also caused by chemicals such as tar from cigarettes.
- Greater exposure – more mutations – greater chance that cell survives – cell will replicate – pass mutation on to daughter cells.
- This mutation remains in the one organism unless it is where sex cells are made.
- Workers with radiation must be shielded and protected – e.g. lead jackets and shielded cubicles of Radiographers, test badges of nuclear power workers.
- **Cancer** – cells lose ability to stop dividing – **grow out of control**.

Genetic engineering

When genes are artificially transferred from one living thing to another – between members of same or different species.

Plasmids
Pieces of bacterial DNA – can have other genes inserted, e.g. human factor 8, human insulin – plasmids carry new gene into bacterial cell – bacteria now makes human product – basis of genetic engineering – this is how human insulin is made.

Benefits

Conquering cystic fibrosis
- Healthy gene could be placed into cell in embryo.
- Replicates and provides the embryo with normal secretions in lungs.
Or
- Same gene could be transferred via virus directly into the lungs of cystic child.
- Virus genetically engineered to carry healthy gene – infects lungs of child – healthy gene transferred and starts to work in child.

Disadvantages

- How far do scientists go?
- Do we clone human beings?
- Do we select the genes of our children?
The moral debate will continue.

Tissue culture

A small group of cells taken from a plant or animal – grown using special media and chemicals such as hormones.

Advantages

Be prepared to write a short essay to discuss advantages and disadvantages of genetic engineering.

- Can produce thousands of identical plants from one small tissue culture.
- All plants genetically identical – **clones**.
- Human or animal cells also grown as tissue cultures – they don't form living things, just sheets of cells – can be used to test drugs etc. – saves using live animals.
- **Embryo transplants** carried out this way – fertilised ovum produces ball of cells – split up – each cell develops into an embryo on its own – vets use technique if farmer wants to produce lots of identical offspring in cattle, pigs or sheep.

Cloning

This is not quite genetic engineering – not altering genes – manipulating cells or cell nuclei – technique used in both plants and animals.

Problems

- Moral questions about human use of cultured embryos.
- Genes in clones all same – can cause problems.
- Lack of variation – evolutionary process has been stopped.
- Wild herds must be kept alive to maintain large number of natural genes for future generations to breed from.
- Cloning is quick and cheap way of breeding.

Be prepared to write a short essay on benefits and problems.

27

LIFE PROCESSES AND LIVING THINGS

Selective breeding

- Humans use knowledge of genetics to select which animals and plants to breed.
- Right choice of animals to breed from could improve herd, e.g.
  – herds of cows that produce more milk
  – pigs that grow bigger
  – disease resistant cereals.

Evolution

- Evidence comes from **fossils** – found in rocks.
- Fossils show us how living things have changed – or stayed same – over millions of years.

Formation of fossils

- Hard parts of animals and plants – do not decay easily – covered by sand/silt – replaced over millions of years by minerals in rocks – animal/plant becomes rock – **fossil**.
- Sometimes soft tissues do not decay – reason? – microbes that cause matter to decay are absent or no oxygen to help decay process etc. – soft tissue then makes fossil.
- Life evolved over 3000 million years ago.
- Living things today evolved from living things from past – life evolved from first simple living things.
- Evolution takes millions of years – many animals and plants have become **extinct**.
- Changes in living things in fossil record – evidence that supports theory of evolution.

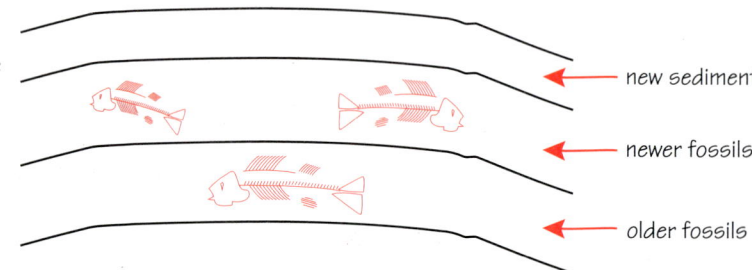

Natural selection

How evolution happens.
- One species of living thing has many individual differences – differences are passed on in parents' genes – from generation to generation by reproduction.

Process of natural selection

- One characteristic very well suited to environment.
- May give that animal or plant and its offspring an advantage.
- Advantage (e.g. camouflage in an insect) means that animal survives – passes on its genes to its offspring.
- Over many generations camouflage may get better and species changes colour or shape – **evolution**.
- Characteristics suited to environment are passed on from one generation to next.
- Living things that 'fit' their environment will survive, those less well adapted could become extinct.

Variation, inheritance and evolution

Questions

1. How many chromosomes are in a human cell nucleus? _____
2. What do you call the 'packages' of information on chromosomes? _____
3. What chemical are chromosomes made from? _____
4. How many chromosomes are there in a human sperm cell? _____
5. How many chromosomes are there in a human ovum? _____
6. What is the chromosome pair for sex determination in a human male? _____
7. What is the chromosome pair for sex determination in a human female? _____
8. Which word describes species of living things which no longer exist? _____

Use the words below to describe the following pairs of genes for questions 9 to 13.
homozygous recessive,   homozygous dominant,   heterozygous

If N is normal and C is recessive custic fibrosis gene:

9. The genotype CC is _____
10. The genotype NC is _____

If B = brown eyes and is dominant, b = blue eyes and is recessive

11. Bb _____
12. BB _____
13. bb _____

14. What gives us the most information about evolution? _____
15. By what process does evolution occur? _____
16. How long ago did life evolve on Earth? _____
17. What are genetically identical living things called? _____
18. What is the name of the process where humans control the breeding of animals? _____
19. What is the process of body cell division called? _____
20. What is the process of sex cell division called? _____
21. What do we call the process where genes are transferred from one living thing to another? _____
22. Which types of radiation cause mutations? _____

LIFE PROCESSES AND LIVING THINGS

Living things and their environment
Adaptation and competition

- Living things live where conditions suit them.
- They are in competition with each other.
- **Population** – group of animals or plants of same species living in same place.
- **Community** – group of populations of different species living in same place, e.g. pond, wood.

Population size

Population size may be affected by **competition** for/with:
- **food** – animals and plants compete for food resources – if successful, will survive to breed
- **space and light** – plants – photosynthesis needs light
  – animals – **carnivore** needs area to live in with enough **prey** animals for food – will often defend this area as its **territory** and drive away any other predators
- **living things** – **herbivores** restrict the growth and populations of plants
  – **carnivores** restrict populations of herbivores and other carnivores
- **humans** – can remove or introduce species – can affect whole food chain – effect may be devastating, e.g. grey squirrel vs. red squirrel
- **disease** – may deplete a population, e.g. myxomatosis kills rabbits.

Human impact on the environment

Air pollution

- **Sulphur dioxide** and **nitrogen oxides**.
- Produced when fossil fuels are burnt in furnaces and engines.
- These gases are dangerous – can cause asthma attacks.
- Gases dissolve in rain water to produce sulphuric acid and nitric acid – **acid rain**.
- This can kill plants – if acid content of rivers and lakes becomes too high, animals and plants cannot survive.

Increasing human population

- Raw materials – **resources** of Earth are being rapidly used up.
- Many resources are **non-renewable**.
- Greater standard of living – resources used faster.
- Leads to more waste – can lead to greater pollution unless there are adequate controls.

Management of Earth's resources and waste produced is one of the biggest problems to solve in the 21st century.

Water pollution

Polluted water can interfere with all of life's processes.
- Amount of O_2, nitrate, phosphate are indicators of water quality.

Pollutants
- Factory waste – may include **acid, cyanide** or metals such as **mercury** and **lead**.
- Acid irritates cells – damages plant roots, fish gills – prevents diffusion of oxygen – kills fish.
- Cyanide – poison of respiratory system – prevents cells from making energy – can kill in seconds – enters food chain.
- Mercury and lead **affect bone** and **nerve cells**.

LIVING THINGS AND THEIR ENVIRONMENT

Fertilisers

- Sprayed onto fields to increase crop production.
- Minerals are soluble – get washed away into rivers and lakes.
- Fertilisers increase growth of **algae** in water.
- Water turns green with algae in badly affected lake.
- Algae absorb light – stops it from reaching plants below surface.
- Bottom-living plants will die.
- Algae die off in winter.
- Dead plants decomposed by bacteria – uses oxygen from water.
- Water depleted in oxygen – animals suffocate and die.
- Bottom-living plants also hold mud with their roots – when they die a lot of mud and silt may be washed down to sea.
- River banks may collapse.
- Whole ecosystem of river or lake may be damaged.

Water becoming deoxygenated by decomposition of dead matter is called **eutrophication**. Polluting water with untreated sewage has the same effect.

Deforestation

- **Plants absorb carbon dioxide during photosynthesis.**
- **Release carbon dioxide** CO_2 during **respiration** – absorb more than they give out.
- Large numbers destroyed – level of CO_2 in air will increase.
- Wood is often burnt – releases more CO_2.
- Tropical rainforests contain enormous number of plants – are being destroyed at an alarming rate.
- Could mean more CO_2 remains in atmosphere.
- Could cause **increased greenhouse effect** – increase in temperature.

Greenhouse effect

- Earth is warm – has insulating layer – this traps some heat from Sun – prevents it from being re-radiated back into space – **greenhouse effect**.
- Water and carbon dioxide part of layer – absorb heat and radiate it back to Earth's surface.
- Has enabled life on Earth to survive.
- Recently has been giving cause for concern.
- Atmosphere has 0.03% of carbon dioxide – level, increasing over recent years – increased burning of fossil fuels – destruction of the tropical rainforests.
- Estimated that doubling CO_2 levels causes rise in temperature of 2 °C.
- Other gases trap heat as well – methane, some chlorofluorocarbons and nitrous oxides.
- Methane produced in intestines of cattle – also produced by rice plants as they grow.
- Producing more rice and beef or milk – increasing levels of methane in atmosphere – adding to greenhouse effect.

Increasing temperature may mean:
- changes in weather – problems with food production
- rise in sea level – problems in coastal areas for all living things – loss of environment.

Weigh up the evidence and form your own opinions. Be prepared to discuss it!

LIFE PROCESSES AND LIVING THINGS

Be prepared to write a short essay on managing food production.

Use of ecosystems

- Organisms used by humans for food — crops grown — animals kept on farms and fish caught in sea.
- Stocks of wild animals used for food can be depleted, e.g. fishing — control number and size of fish caught — no control — fish population may crash — valuable food source lost for many years.

Careful management of natural stocks is needed and this may be achieved by governments co-operating to:

- agree quotas or limits on number of animals removed from wild each year
- be selective in which animals taken, e.g. only take non-breeding adult animals, not young or breeding animals
- avoid animal's breeding season — do not use breeding areas for fishing or hunting.

Artificial ecosystems

Those created by humans — amount of food produced in these areas kept very high by:
- using fertilisers
- using pesticides and fungicides to destroy pests
- reducing competition with wild animals and plants by various means
- bringing extra water by irrigation channels from reservoirs
- selectively breeding better animals and plants that are disease-resistant or grow bigger or faster
- using genetic engineering to produce disease-resistant crops.

Can have major effect on natural ecosystems — natural world needs consideration before farmland created.
All domestic animals need to be treated in humane way while growing, being transported and when killed.

Efficient artificial ecosystems

- Using short food chains — short food chain, less energy lost between links in chain.
- Food animals lose energy when move around — if movement restricted animals will grow faster — reason behind factory farming. Is it humane? Is it necessary?
- Controlling temperature — heating areas reduces heat lost by animals.

Energy and nutrient transfer

Producers
Sun is source of energy for all life on Earth.

- Green plants — capture the energy from Sun.
- Store energy in cells.
- Some energy used — growth and repair, making protein, fat etc.
- Some lost as waste.

Consumers

- Animals — some eat plants, some eat animals.
- Energy of plant or animal taken in.
- Energy used for repair, growth, making proteins, e.g. hormones, enzymes.
- Respiration produces energy for living processes.

LIVING THINGS AND THEIR ENVIRONMENT

Consumers

- Animals – some eat plants, some eat animals.
- Energy of plant or animal taken in.
- Energy used for repair, growth, making proteins, e.g. hormones, enzymes.
- Respiration produces energy for living processes.
- Energy lost in faeces – also as waste from chemical reactions in cells.
- Energy lost as heat – animals produce heat as they move – heat energy lost to air.
- **Mammals** and **birds** lose more energy this way – **warm blooded** – **homoiothermic**.

Decomposers

- Microbes – bacteria and fungi.
- Dead materials completely decomposed – all energy originally captured by plant back into environment.

Pollution enters food chain

E.g.
- **mercury** builds up in plant tissue
- fish eat plants – mercury in diet
- mercury level builds up in fish – may kill fish
- fish eaten by predator, e.g. otter or pike
- these top consumers get high doses of mercury in diet – eventually kills them.

Often top consumer dies – levels of poison may not be high enough in producer or primary consumer – level increases further along the food chain you go – often reaches lethal levels at final predator.

Food webs

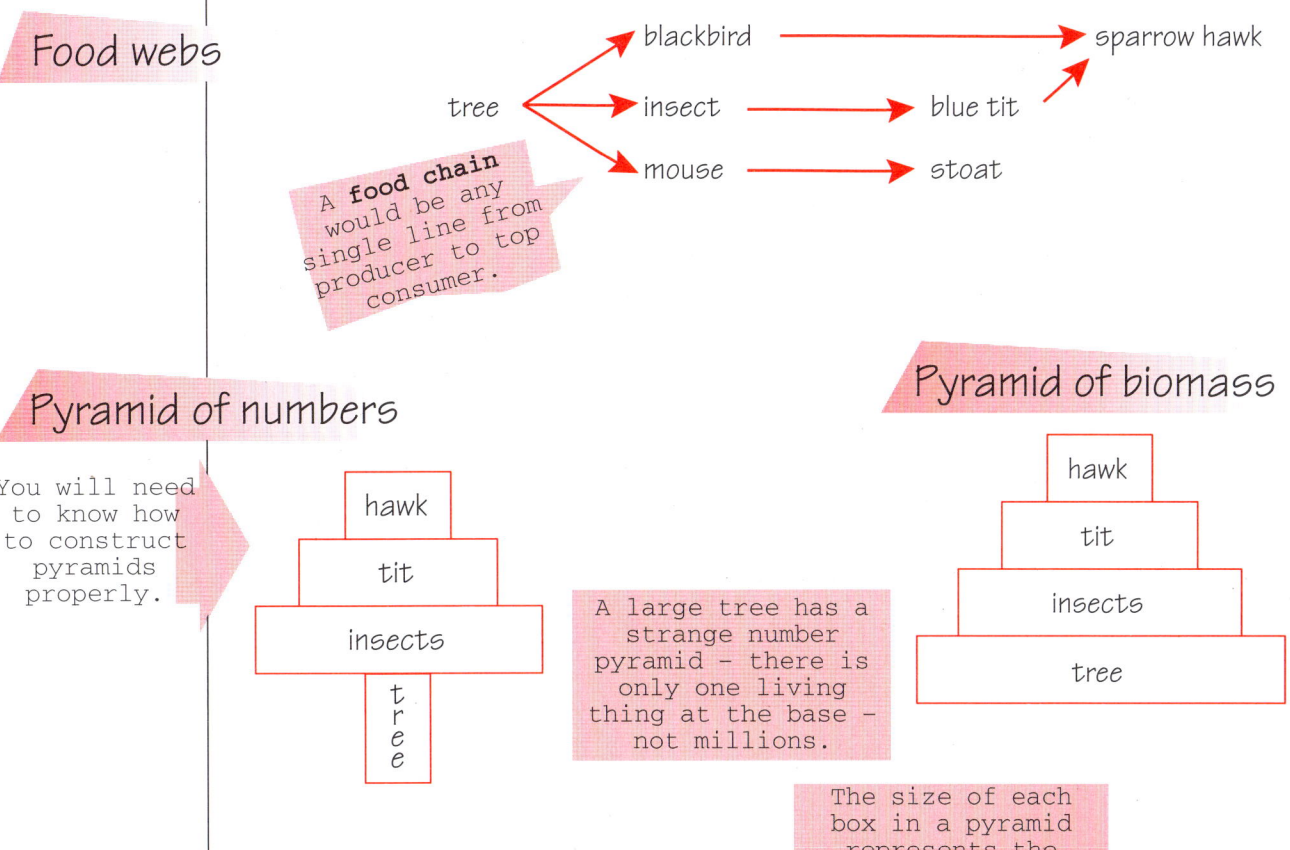

A **food chain** would be any single line from producer to top consumer.

Pyramid of numbers

You will need to know how to construct pyramids properly.

A large tree has a strange number pyramid – there is only one living thing at the base – not millions.

Pyramid of biomass

The size of each box in a pyramid represents the number of individuals or amount of biomass at that level.

33

LIFE PROCESSES AND LIVING THINGS

Important – you must mention role of bacteria/fungi in C and N cycles.

Carbon cycle

- **Carbon** in **carbohydrate**, **protein** and **fat**.
- Plants get their carbon from air – carbon dioxide (CO_2).
- Use it to make food – photosynthesis – build proteins, fats and carbohydrates. 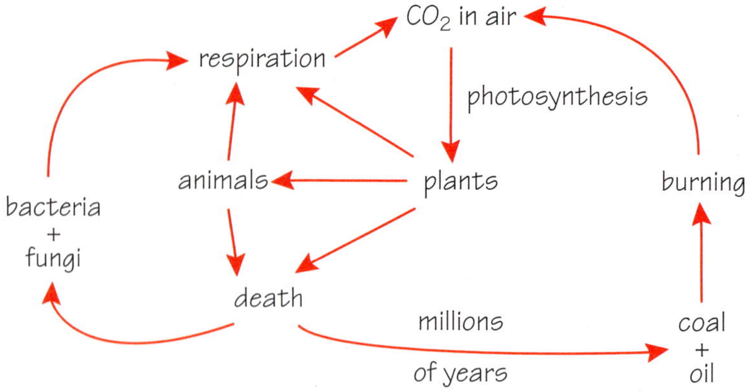
- Animals get carbon by eating plants and other animals.
- Respiration – uses food – releases carbon dioxide back into air.
- Plants **take in** carbon dioxide – animals give out carbon dioxide.
- Plants and animals die – bodies decompose.
- Dead matter broken down by bacteria and other microbes – decomposers – carbon into their bodies.
- Decomposers also respire – carbon dioxide into air.
- Burning – releases carbon dioxide into air – extra carbon dioxide.

Nitrogen cycle

- Nitrogen (N_2) needed to make **proteins**.
- Proteins build animal and plant tissue.
- Plants build proteins – take **nitrate** out of soil through roots.
- Animals eat plants – break down plant protein – build up animal protein.
- Animals excrete **urea and faeces** – contains nitrogen waste.
- Animals and plants die – the nitrogen can be returned to the cycle.
- Decomposing bacteria break the protein/urea/faeces down into ammonia (nitrogen + hydrogen).
- **Nitrifying bacteria** change this ammonia to nitrate (nitrogen + oxygen).
- Plant roots absorb nitrate – cycle again.
- **Denitrifying bacteria** – change nitrate into nitrogen gas.
- **Nitrogen fixing bacteria** – take nitrogen out of air – build it into nitrates. These bacteria can be found by themselves in soil, or living in roots of plants belonging to pea and bean family, e.g. clover, peas etc. These plants are called **legumes**.

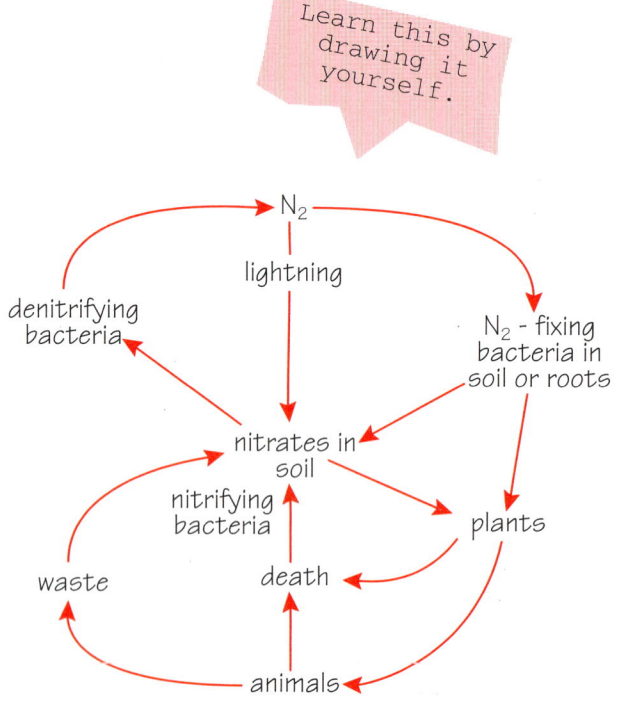

Learn this by drawing it yourself.

Living things and their environment

Questions

1. What is contained in fertiliser that seriously pollutes rivers? _____
2. Why do living things need carbon? _____
3. Why do living things need nitrogen? _____
4. Where do most plants get their nitrogen? _____
5. Where do herbivores get their nitrogen for amino acids? _____
6. Where do carnivores get their nitrogen? _____
7. What is the name of the microbes that change nitrate into nitrogen gas? _____
8. What is the name of the microbes that change nitrogen gas into nitrate? _____
9. What is the end product of urine breakdown by nitrifying bacteria? _____
10. Which raw materials are used by plants to make amino acids during photosynthesis? _____
11. Where do plants get their carbon from? _____
12. Where do animals get their carbon from? _____
13. What is the waste product of plant respiration? _____
14. What is the waste product of animal respiration? _____
15. What percentage of the air is carbon dioxide? _____
16. Which type of microbes live in the root nodules of legumes? _____
17. Which gas is mainly responsible for destructive 'acid rain'? _____
18. Which gases are responsible for the 'greenhouse effect'? _____
19. Rain is often naturally slightly acid. Which gas is responsible for 'natural' acid rain? _____
20. Which gases are the major pollutants from coal fired power stations? _____
21. Which pollutant will damage the gills of fish? _____
22. Which poison prevents cells from making energy? _____
23. Which heavy metal has been linked to nerve damage in inner city school children? _____
24. Which heavy metal can make bones very brittle as well as causing nerve damage? _____

Answers

Life processes and living things

Life processes and cell activity

1 Botany 2 Zoology 3 Sensitivity 4 Respiration 5 Excretion
6 Elimination or egestion 7 Reproduction 8 Growth 9 Oxygen
10 Respiration 11 Movement – respiration – sensitivity – feeding – excretion – reproduction – growth 12 MRSFERG 13 Cytoplasm 14 Nucleus
15 Cellulose cell wall 16 Chloroplast 17 Vacuole 18 Tissue 19 Organ
20 System 21 Organism 22 Vacuole – cellulose – chlorophyll 23 Cell
24 Organ 25 Organ

Humans as organisms

1 Carbohydrate, protein, fat 2 Peristalsis
3 Kills germs and creates best conditions for enzymes to work
4 Emulsifies fats – increases surface area of fat globules for enzymes to work on
5 Digests protein 6 Right ventricle 7 Left ventricle
8 Withstand high blood pressure 9 Keep blood travelling the right way – prevent backflow 10 Carry oxygen 11 Urea, carbon dioxide, any food, hormones
12 Walls of alveoli 13 Aerobic 14 Anaerobic 15 Stimulus → receptor → coordinator → effector → response 16 Brain and spinal cord 17 Insulin
18 Glucagon 19 FSH 20 LH 21 Broken down to urea by liver 22 More permeable to water – water reabsorbed back into blood – concentrated urine produced 23 Bacteria – larger – more genes – can survive on their own. Viruses – much smaller – few genes + protein – only grow inside living cells
24 Nicotine

Green plants as organisms

1 Chlorophyll – in chloroplasts 2 Palisade mesophyll 3 Xylem 4 Phloem
5 Xylem 6 Bright light 7 Dark/cloudy 8 Warm/windy 9 Cold/wet/still
10 Summer 11 Diffusion 12 Osmosis 13 Turgid 14 Plasmolysed
15 Nitrate 16 Phosphate 17 Potassium 18 Potassium 19 Phosphate
20 Nitrate 21 Grow towards 22 Grow towards 23 Grow away

Variation, inheritance and evolution

1 46 2 Genes 3 DNA 4 23 5 23 6 XY 7 XX 8 Extinct
9 Homozygous recessive 10 Heterozygous 11 Heterozygous
12 Homozygous dominant 13 Homozygous recessive 14 Fossils 15 Natural selection 16 Over 3000 million years 17 Clones 18 Selective breeding
19 Mitosis 20 Meiosis 21 Genetic engineering 22 Ultra-violet, X-ray, gamma

Living things and their environment

1 Nitrate/phosphate 2 'building brick' of all molecules of life 3 To make proteins
4 Nitrate 5 Plants 6 Other animals 7 Denitrifiers 8 Nitrogen fixers
9 Ammonia 10 Nitrate, carbon dioxide, water 11 Carbon dioxide 12 Plants
13 Carbon dioxide 14 Carbon dioxide 15 0.03% 16 Nitrogen fixers
17 Sulphur dioxide 18 Carbon dioxide and methane 19 Carbon dioxide
20 Sulphur dioxide and nitrogen oxides 21 Sulphur dioxide as acid rain
22 Cyanide 23 Lead 24 Mercury

Materials and their properties

Classifying materials and considering reactions

States of matter

- Matter occurs in three forms (or states) called: **solids, liquids and gases**.
- All matter consists of very tiny particles. These are the smallest bits of a substance that you can get.

The particles:
- are very small and not destroyed in physical or chemical changes
- attract each other when they are close together
- move and the movement increases as matter is heated.

Changes of State happen when the different states are heated or cooled.

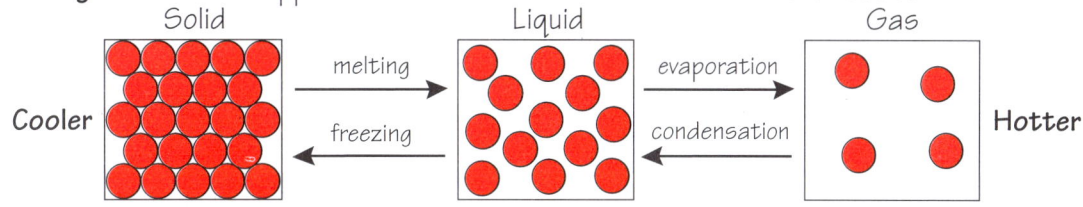

Cooler — Solid —melting→ Liquid —evaporation→ Gas — Hotter
Solid ←freezing— Liquid ←condensation— Gas

- **Melting** – particles of solid get more energy from heating so vibrate more and push apart from each other – attraction reduces until they are able to move.
- **Evaporating** – some particles of a liquid have more energy than others – move faster – particles with energy to escape the attraction of others can escape from the liquid → gas (vapour) – rest have reduced energy – cooler liquid.
- **Boiling** – all the liquid particles have enough energy to escape so evaporation is much faster.
- **Diffusing** – gases spread out and completely mix with each other – happens because particles move rapidly at random and are spaced out.
- **Dissolving** – when a solute completely mixes into a solvent (often liquid) – happens when moving liquid particles break apart the solute particles.
- **Expansion** – heating makes particles move faster – push apart – matter gets bigger.

Elements, compounds and mixtures

Elements – simplest sort of matter which exists – can't be made simpler – contain **only** atoms of one type – about 90 naturally occurring elements, e.g. iron, sulphur, sodium, chlorine.

Compounds – when two or more elements chemically bond together
- compounds have different properties to the elements
- can be separated only by chemical reactions
- compounds have fixed melting and boiling points.

Mixtures – two or more elements or compounds not chemically combined together
- behave the same as the elements or compounds
- can be separated by physical processes
- melting point varies with various ratios of content.

Atomic Structure

- Matter contains particles called **atoms**.
- If the matter contains only one kind of atom, it is called an **element**.

MATERIALS AND THEIR PROPERTIES

- Elements behave differently because different atoms behave differently.
- Atoms are different because they have different structures.
- Atoms' structures are made of even tinier atomic particles.

The mass of 1 means protons and neutrons have same mass.

atomic particles	symbol	mass	charge
protons	p	1	+1
neutrons	n	1	0
electrons	e	negligible	−1

Protons and electrons have opposite charges so they attract.

The nucleus is not a control centre as in a cell.

Protons and **neutrons** contained in **nucleus** — surrounded by **electrons** in **shells** — in between is just empty space — see diagram below.

Atoms are represented by this sort of symbol:

(A) mass number
(Z) atomic number

symbol   e.g. $^{23}_{11}Na$ p = 11, e = 11, n = (23 − 11) = 12

Data Book has proton numbers and mass numbers.

How many particles?

Check that you can work out the particles and the electron arrangement in the first twenty elements.

- **protons** — given by proton number (atomic number)
  — each element has its own type of atoms with its own proton number
- **electrons** — same number as number of protons
  — atom is neutral — opposite charges balance out
- **neutrons** — found by taking atomic proton number away from mass number
  — **mass number** is particles in nucleus (protons + neutrons)
- **Isotopes** are same type of atom — same protons — different number of neutrons:
  e.g. $^{35}_{17}Cl$ (17p, 18n); $^{37}_{17}Cl$ (17p, 20n)   isotopes of chlorine

Arrangement of electrons:

- electrons arranged in shells — have different energy levels
- electrons go in available shell with lowest energy level — nearest to nucleus
- shells fill with different numbers of electrons
  — then not available to take more
- maximum number — 1st shell (2)
  — 2nd shell (8)
  — 3rd shell (8)
- Na — 11 electrons — 2 go in 1st shell (full)
  — 8 in second shell (full)
  — 1 in third shell.

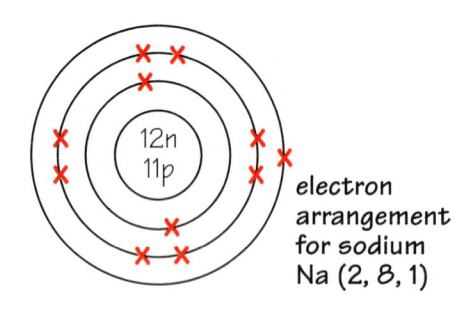

electron arrangement for sodium Na (2, 8, 1)

Hazard symbols

Hazard symbols — used to show dangerous substances

You need to recognise, explain and give an example of these.

Oxidising
provides oxygen—
helps burning
e.g. potassium nitrate

Harmful
similar to toxic but less dangerous
e.g. copper sulphate

Toxic
can kill if swallowed or absorbed
e.g. mercury

Highly flammable
catches fire easily
e.g. alcohol (ethanol)

Corrosive
attack and destroy eyes and skin
e.g. nitric acid

Irritant
harm skin but not corrosive
e.g. calcium oxide

CLASSIFYING MATERIALS AND CONSIDERING REACTIONS

Bonding

- Some atoms are unwilling to react – **noble gases** – see **Periodic Table**.
- Have a very stable structure – highest occupied energy level (outer shell) is full.
- Other elements react in order to get a similar electronic arrangement.
- They have to **gain or lose electrons** to obtain a **full outer shell**.
- Bonding happens when atoms cooperate so that both become more stable – different bonding depending on **how** the atoms cooperate.

Ionic bonding

- Happens between metal atoms – try to lose electrons
  and non-metal atoms – try to gain electrons
  e.g. sodium and chlorine:

Note where ion charge goes.

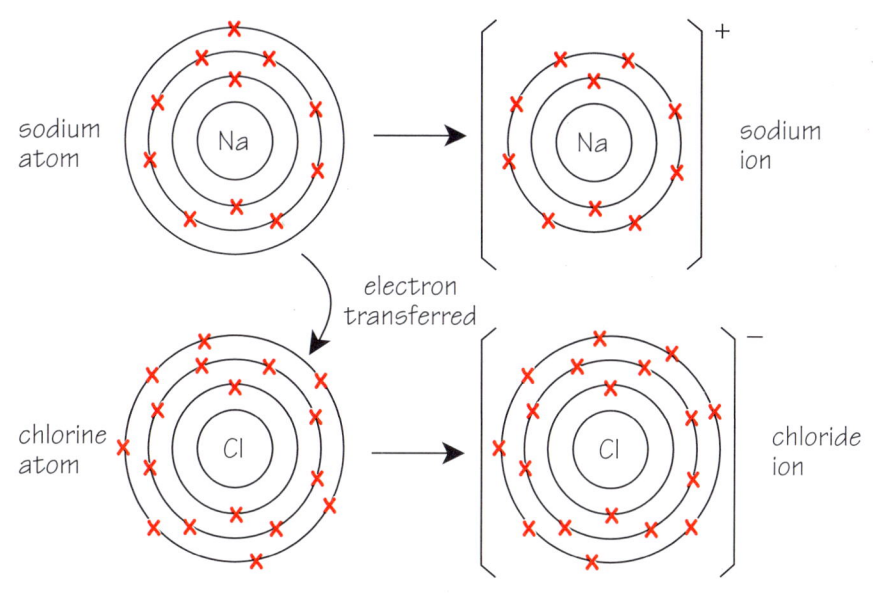

sodium atom → sodium ion

electron transferred

chlorine atom → chloride ion

- Ions form when atoms lose or gain electrons to get full outer shell.
- Because protons and electrons are no longer equal – ions produced have an electrical charge.

Data Book has charges of common ions.

Na (2,8,1) loses e^- → Na^+ (2,8)   Cl (2,8,7) gains e^- → Cl^- (2,8,8)
($11p^+ = 11\ e^-$)   ($11p^+ > 10e^-$)   ($17p^+ = 17e^-$)   ($17p^+ < 18e^-$)

- **Metals lose electrons** – form positive ions $Mg \rightarrow Mg^{2+} + 2e^-$ $Ca \rightarrow Ca^{2+} + 2e^-$
- **Non-metals gain electrons** – form negative ions $O + 2e^- \rightarrow O^{2-}$ $F + e^- \rightarrow F^-$

- The ions formed have the electronic structure of one of the noble gases
  e.g. Na^+ (2,8) – electronic structure of Ne (2,8)
       Cl^- (2,8,8) – electronic structure of Ar (2,8,8)

- **Oppositely charged ions attract strongly** to form an orderly **giant structure**.
- This structure – called an **ionic lattice** is the actual compound formed.
- Sodium chloride (compound) contains equal numbers of Na^+ and Cl^- – makes a neutral compound – formula NaCl.

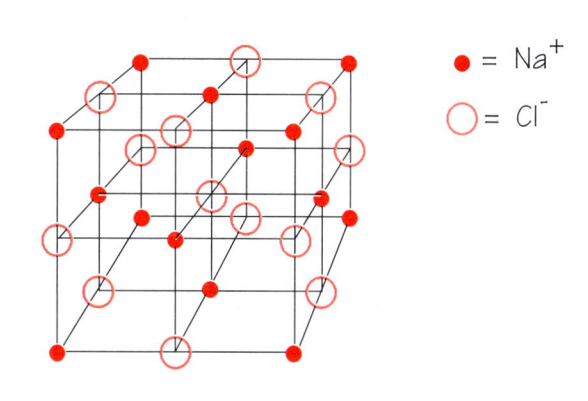

● = Na^+
○ = Cl^-

MATERIALS AND THEIR PROPERTIES

- Strong attraction – needs much energy to get ions to separate in melting.
- Compounds containing ions have high melting points and boiling points.
- Ions become free to move if the strong attraction is broken down by being melted – requires quite a high temperature – being dissolved, they often are soluble in water.
- When molten or in solution ions are free to move – charged ions carry electric charge – ions changed at electrodes by gaining or losing electrons – **Electrolysis**.

Covalent bonding

- Non-metal atoms try to gain electrons to get a full outer shell – become stable.
- They bond together by **sharing pairs of electrons** – called a **single covalent bond**.
- The strong covalent bonds hold the atoms together in a particle called a **molecule**, e.g. hydrogen and chlorine.

Show outer shell only.

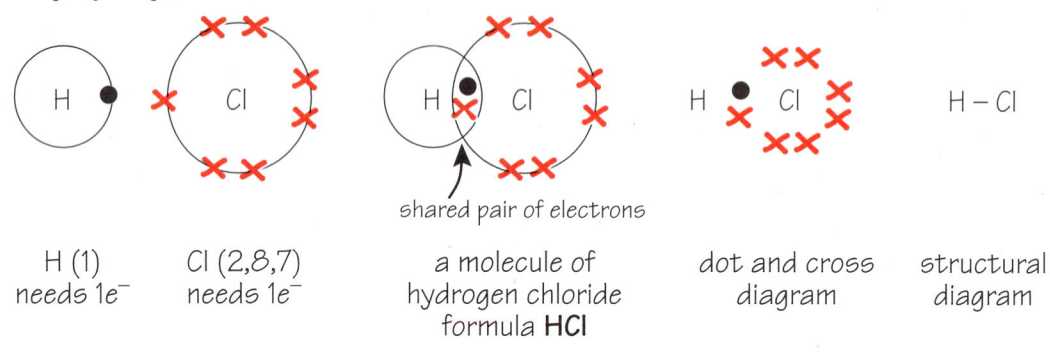

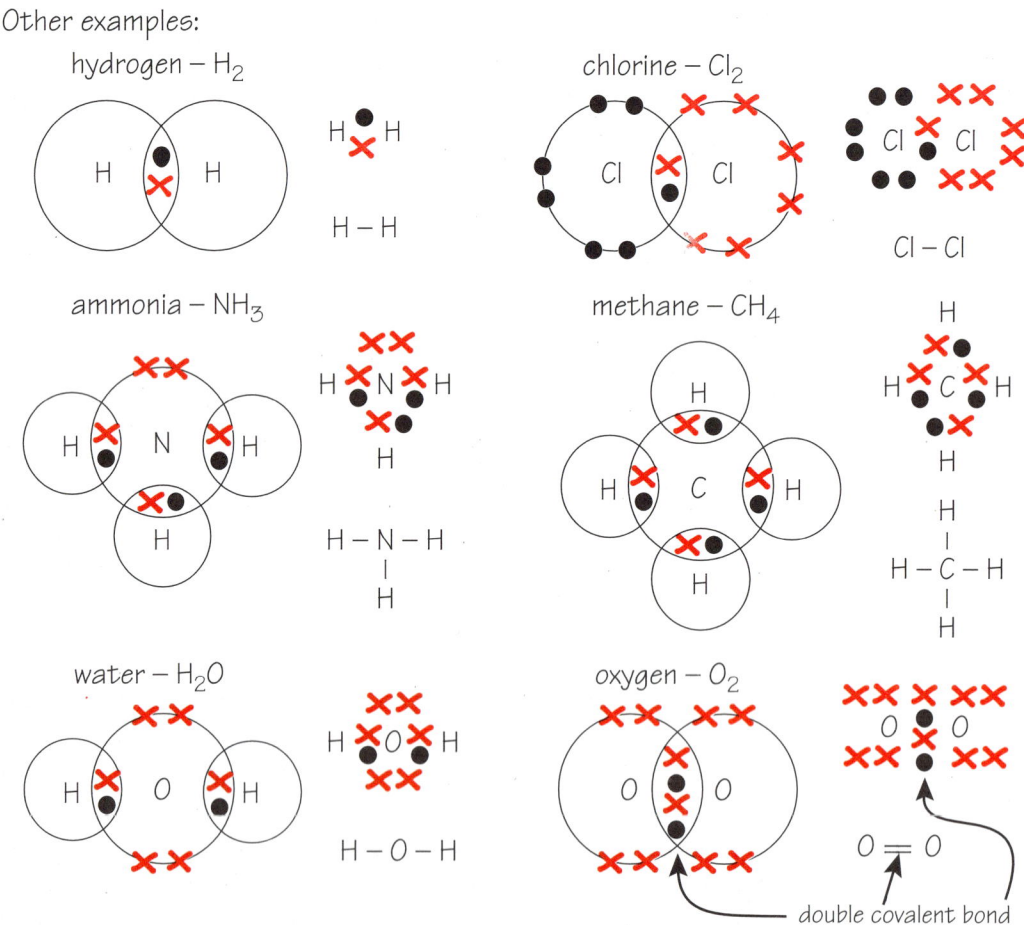

H (1) needs 1e⁻   Cl (2,8,7) needs 1e⁻   a molecule of hydrogen chloride formula **HCl**   dot and cross diagram   structural diagram

shared pair of electrons

Other examples:

hydrogen – H_2 chlorine – Cl_2

H–H   Cl–Cl

ammonia – NH_3 methane – CH_4

H–N–H
  |
  H

H–C–H (with H above and below)

water – H_2O oxygen – O_2

H–O–H   O=O

double covalent bond

See also in **Useful products from oil**.

*Be clear about melting. **Covalent bonds are not broken during melting.** Melting occurs when very weak forces of attraction **between molecules** are overcome and molecules are able to move about.*

- Molecules are **neutral** (not charged) – very weak attractive forces between them.
- Compounds containing **small molecules** have low melting and boiling points – often liquids or gases at room temperature.
- Do not conduct electricity – no charged ions to carry current.

40

CLASSIFYING MATERIALS AND CONSIDERING REACTIONS

Very large molecules – macromolecules

- Covalent bonding can lead to large molecules – particularly carbon compounds.
- Plastics contain long chain molecules – called polymers.
- Long chains tangle up – harder to separate when heated – higher melting points.
- Substances are plastic – means softens as heated – chains untangle with heat.
- Some can be repeatedly softened and hardened – called **thermosoftening** plastics – these can be remoulded and so reused (recycled) e.g. polythene.
- Some are soft when made but when they first cool the chains tangle up and form extra strong covalent bonds between adjacent chains – cross-linkages.
- Extra bonds mean the chains form a rigid structure which is not softened by heating – called **thermosetting** plastics, e.g. bakelite – useful in higher temperature devices.

Giant covalent structures

- A **giant atomic lattice** is formed when millions of atoms are joined together by strong covalent bonds.
- Substances such as silica (silicon dioxide), graphite (carbon) and diamond (carbon) consist of giant atomic lattices.
- Because the whole structure is held together by strong covalent bonds (i.e. no separate molecules) they have very high melting points.

Diamond and **graphite** – both forms of the element carbon:
- contain only carbon atoms which are covalently bonded in a giant structure
- have different properties and uses because of the difference in these structures.

substance	diamond	graphite
structure	(● = C atom)	layer 1, layer 2 — weak bond
bonding	each atom strongly bonded to four others by strong covalent bonds.	each atom strongly bonded to three others forming layers – weak bonds between layers
strength	very tough – hardest natural substance – rigid atomic lattice	soft – layers can slide over each other – weak bonds between layers break easily
electrical conduction	does not conduct – all electrons involved in strong bonds	good conductor – electrons in weak bonds between layers can move
appearance	transparent, crystalline solid	black, shiny opaque solid
uses	cutting tools – drills, jewellery	pencil leads – soft, electrical contacts

- Silicon dioxide – structure similar to diamonds – rigid, tough, high melting point.

Metallic bonding

- Metal atoms want to lose electrons to become stable.
- The electrons which are lost are from the highest occupied energy level – outer shell.
- Metallic bonding is where the metal atoms lose these electrons and so become positively charged ions and the electrons are in the spaces between the ions.

These free electrons:
- hold the structure strongly together in an orderly arrangement because of the opposite charges – metals are tough and usually have quite high melting points

MATERIALS AND THEIR PROPERTIES

- allow the metal ions to move past each other and still retain the bonding strength — so metals are malleable — can be bent, twisted and pulled without breaking
- in alloys (mixtures of metals with other elements) other atoms prevent the metal atoms moving about so easily — alloy becomes tougher — **useful**
- can move through the metal so carrying an electric current — conductors
- enable heat energy to quickly pass through the metal — good conductors of heat.

Electrolysis

- A chemical reaction caused by electricity — direct current.
- A substance containing ions is made liquid by dissolving in water or by melting — **electrolyte**.
- Electricity (direct current) is passed through the solution or molten substance by means of electrodes.
- Electrolyte breaks down (decomposes) into elements. Released as gases or deposited as metals at the electrodes.
- Because ions are in solution or liquid they are free to move towards the charged electrodes.
- Negative ions attract to positive anode — lose electrons — become atoms eg $Cl^- - e^- \rightarrow Cl$ losing electrons is called **oxidation** (**o**xidation **i**s **l**oss).
- Positive ions attract to negative cathode — gain electrons — become atoms, e.g. $Na^+ + e^- \rightarrow Na$ gaining electrons is called **reduction** (**r**eduction **i**s **g**ain).
- Oxidation and reduction happen together — called **Redox** reactions.

Remember **OILRIG**.

Before current is on

positive electrode (anode) negative electrode (cathode)

When current is on

Extraction from raw materials

- Molten sodium chloride produces chlorine gas at the anode and sodium metal as a liquid at the cathode.
- Sodium chloride solution produces chlorine, hydrogen and sodium hydroxide.
- Aluminium oxide produces aluminium and oxygen.

Electroplating

- An object is coated with a thin layer of metal by electrolysis.
- The object (e.g. metal coffee pot) is connected as the negative electrode.
- Electrolyte contains ions of the metal to be put on — plated, e.g. silver.
- Electrolysis — metal from electrolyte deposits on the negative electrode. E.g. silver deposits all over the metal coffee pot — it has been electroplated.

Purifying metals

- Some metals need purifying after extraction, e.g. copper for wiring needs to be pure.

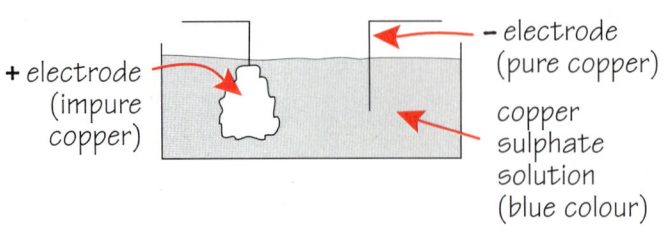

+ electrode (impure copper)

− electrode (pure copper)

copper sulphate solution (blue colour)

impurities   pure copper

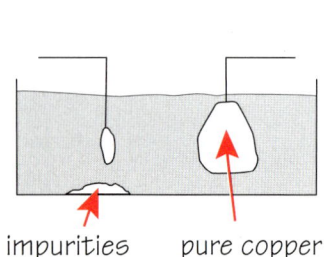

Set up at start   Set up after electrolysis

42

CLASSIFYING MATERIALS AND CONSIDERING REACTIONS

- The copper from the impure electrode goes into the solution as ions
  $$Cu_{(s)} - 2e^- \rightarrow Cu^{2+}_{(aq)}$$
- The copper ions in solution get deposited on the negative electrode — pure copper
  $$Cu^{2+}_{(aq)} + 2e^- \rightarrow Cu_{(s)}$$

Representing reactions

In any chemical change (**reaction**) the starting substances (**reactants**) become new substances (**products**).

- Shown as a diagram called a **chemical equation**:
  reactants → products (the arrow means 'changes into').

> Equations are diagrams not sentences – must have two sides.

- When the names of the substances are put in, it is called a **word equation**,
  e.g. methane + oxygen → carbon dioxide + water (+ means 'and').

- Reactions happen between particles of substances.
- Represent the particles by a **formula**.
- **Elements** – represented by symbols,
  e.g. iron – Fe, sulphur – S – **one atom** of the element
       2Fe – 2 atoms of iron **not bonded** together.

> Remember numbers mean different things depending on where placed
> e.g.
> 2Fe = Fe + Fe
> Cl$_2$ means Cl – Cl.

> Make sure you use the capital and small case letters in the correct way.

- Some element gases and bromine have a formula showing **two atoms bonded**,
  e.g. H_2; O_2; N_2; Cl_2; Br_2; F_2 – these are diatomic molecules.

> Learn these.

Compounds – formula shows smallest amount possible and what it contains,
  e.g. sodium chloride – formula **NaCl** – one sodium (**Na**) joined to one chlorine (**Cl**),
  e.g. methane – formula **CH$_4$** – one carbon (**C**) joined to four hydrogens (**H$_4$**),
  e.g. **3NaCl** – three separate units of sodium chloride.

> Note that the number 1 is not shown since symbol stands for one atom.

Writing formulae

Ionic compounds – contain positive and negative charged ions.

- Formula shows ions in same order as name.
- Amount of each ion will balance opposite charges – charges not usually shown,
  e.g. calcium oxide – contains Ca^{2+} and O^{2-} – need **one of each** to balance charge
       – so formula – **CaO**,
  e.g. potassium sulphate – contains K^+ and SO_4^{2-} – need **two** K^+ for each **one** SO_4^{2-}
       – so formula K_2SO_4
  e.g. iron (III) chloride – contains Fe^{3+} and Cl^- – need **one** Fe^{3+} for each **three** Cl^-
       – so formula $FeCl_3$.

Covalent compounds – contain molecules – formulae not easy to work out.

Examples:

water	H_2O	sulphur dioxide	SO_2	methane	CH_4
nitrogen dioxide	NO_2	alcohol	C_2H_5OH	nitrogen monoxide	NO
carbon dioxide	CO_2	carbon monoxide	CO	ammonia	NH_3

> Learn these common ones for the exam.

Reading equations

- If the formula is put in for each of the reactants and products – formula equation,
  e.g. word equation   lithium + water → lithium hydroxide + hydrogen
       formula equation $2Li_{(s)}$ + $2H_2O_{(l)}$ → $2LiOH_{(aq)}$ + $H_{2(g)}$

MATERIALS AND THEIR PROPERTIES

The symbols in brackets are **state symbols** – give the state of the substance:
(s) – solid ; (l) – liquid ; (g) – gas ; (aq) – dissolved in water –aqueous.

Balancing equations

When the formulae are put in for each of the substances in a word equation:

e.g. zinc + sulphuric acid → zinc sulphate + hydrogen
      Zn   + H_2SO_4 → $ZnSO_4$ + H_2

The particles represented by the formulae can be worked out on each side
e.g. 1–Zn(1 atom of zinc) 2–H, 1–S, 4–O → 1–Zn, 1–S, 4–O, 2–H

You can see that the atoms involved are exactly the same on each side
- An equation like this is said to be **balanced.**
- All equations should be balanced because they represent reactions and in a chemical reaction atoms cannot be created or destroyed.
- The atoms that are shown in the reactants must also be present in the products no more and no less.

This sometimes does not show correctly in the equation when it is first written,

e.g.   magnesium + hydrochloric acid → magnesium chloride + hydrogen
        Mg   + HCl   → $MgCl_2$ + H_2
counting atoms 1–Mg   1–H, 1–Cl   → 1–Mg, 2–Cl   2–H

the products contain **one more H** and **one more Cl** than the reactants. This is not possible – the equation is **unbalanced**.

> You cannot change the formulae to balance an equation.

To balance the equation the reactants need to have these extra atoms – **one more H** and **one more Cl** – in other words **one more unit of HCl** – so need 2HCl in reactants.

> Hint – when balancing equations always make the lesser side more – you cannot make the bigger side less.

This is shown in the **balanced equation**
        Mg + 2HCl → $MgCl_2$ + H_2

Reactions in electrolysis

- Reaction happens at each electrode – each is represented by a **half-equation**.
- Each half-equation has to be balanced and they must balance with each other
  e.g. in the electrolysis of sodium chloride solution.

At the positive electrode negative chloride ions lose electrons and are released as chlorine gas:

$Cl^- - e^- \rightarrow Cl_{2(g)}$ – unbalanced
$2Cl^- - 2e^- \rightarrow Cl_{2(g)}$ – balanced

At the negative electrode positive hydrogen ions gain electrons and become hydrogen gas:

$2H^+ + 2e^- \rightarrow H_{2(g)}$ – balanced

The half-equations are also balanced with each other – they require the same electrons.

In the electrolysis of aluminium oxide

$2O^{2-} - 4e^- \rightarrow O_{2(g)}$ – balanced
$Al^{3+} + 3e^- \rightarrow Al_{(l)}$ – balanced

Although the half-equations are each balanced they are not balanced with each other – they require different numbers of electrons – not possible in an electrical circuit.

To balance need: $6O^{2-} - 12e^- \rightarrow 3O_{2(g)}$
                  $4Al^{3+} + 12e^- \rightarrow 4Al_{(l)}$

Energy transfer in reactions

Remember these

exit – go **out**
exothermic –
heat given **out**

entrance – go **in**
endothermic –
heat taken **in**.

When a chemical reaction happens energy is always involved.
- When a fuel burns it reacts with oxygen and a lot of heat **energy is released**.
- Reactions like this – **give out energy** to the surroundings – **exothermic**.
- When calcium carbonate is turned into calcium oxide it needs **to be heated** strongly.
- Reactions like this – **take in energy** from something – **endothermic**.

These ideas can be represented as diagrams:

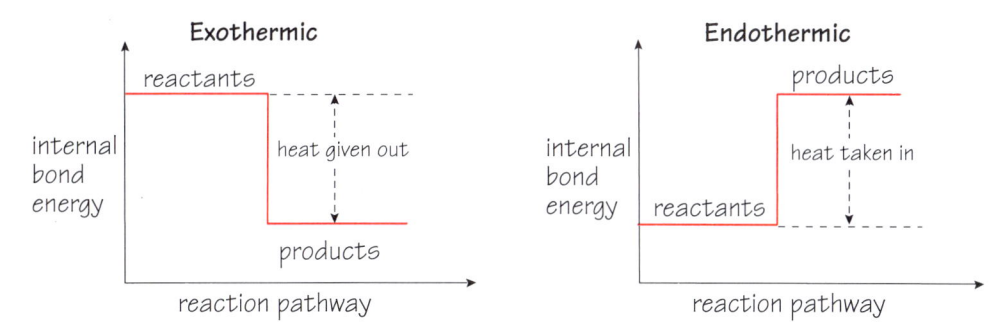

Exothermic: products – less energy than reactants – energy has to be given out

Endothermic: products – more energy than reactants – energy has to be taken in

Any reaction involves reactant particles breaking up and rearranging to form products.
- When bonds are broken – energy is needed – endothermic.
- When bonds are formed – energy is released – exothermic (becomes more stable).
- So reaction path way is actually more complex.

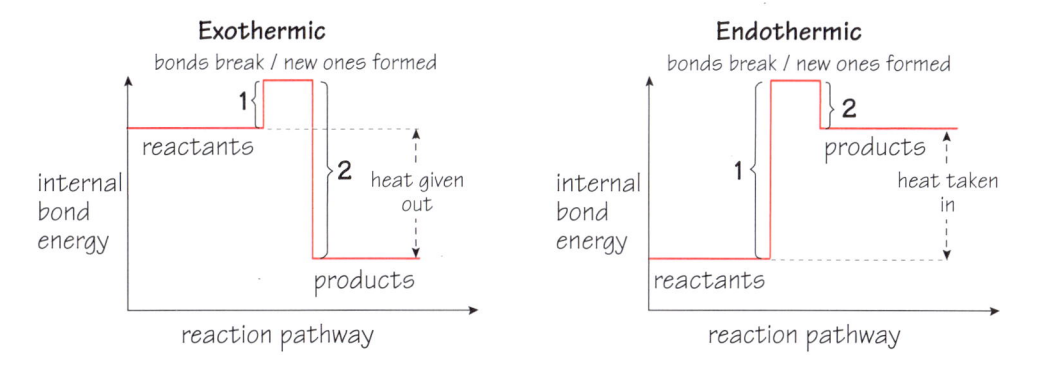

1 – energy needed to break reactant bonds – **activation energy**
2 – energy released as product bonds form

- If **1** is less than **2** – exothermic   if **1** is greater than **2** – endothermic

Using bond energies – if these are given then **1** and **2** can be worked out for a reaction:

e.g. $N_{2(g)} + 3H_{2(g)} \rightleftharpoons 2NH_{3(g)}$ (Haber process)

bond energies (N≡N 945 kJ) (H–H 436 kJ) (N–H 391 kJ) – per mole.

1 energy to break reactant bonds   **2** energy released when product forms
  = 945 + 3 × 436   = 2 × 3 × 391
  = 2253 kJ   = 2346 kJ

The difference (2346 – 2253 = 93 kJ) is released overall – reaction is **exothermic**.

$\Delta H = -93$ kJ/mol (ΔH is the change in energy)

Heat released in industrial processes is valuable and is used as much as possible.

45

Rates of reaction

Any chemical reaction involves new substances (products) being formed.

reactant → products

If we study the reaction between calcium carbonate (in the form of marble chips) and dilute hydrochloric acid:

calcium carbonate + hydrochloric acid → calcium chloride + carbon dioxide + water

$CaCO_{3(s)} + 2HCl_{(aq)} \rightarrow CaCl_{2(aq)} + CO_{2(g)} + H_2O$

If the decreasing reactants are measured — or — If an increasing product is measured,

A graph of the reactants against time   A graph of the products against time

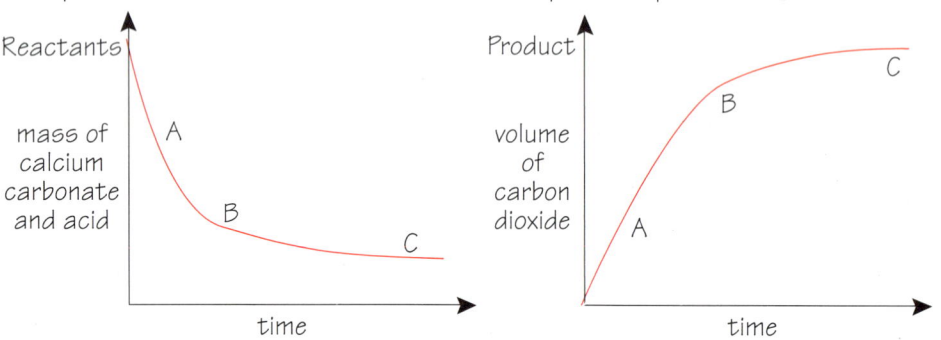

On the graph of volume of carbon dioxide against time at points **A**, **B** and **C**:

A The product increases from zero producing a straight line this means the product is increasing regularly for each unit of time so rate of reaction is constant.

$$\text{Rate} = \frac{\text{increase of product}}{\text{increase in time}}$$

B The line curves gradually towards the horizontal so gradually less product per unit of time — reaction slows down — rate decreases.

C Horizontal line shows no increase in product — reaction has finished — rate is zero.

Reactions in particle terms

- Reactants (and products) consist of particles — these rearrange during a reaction.
- Reactant particles come into contact — by moving and colliding.
- If energy of colliding particles exceeds the **activation energy** — bonds break in reactant particles.
- Broken bonds can rejoin in a different way to form a new substance (product) or in the same way to reform the reactants.

So the rate depends on **how frequently collisions, which have enough energy, take place.**

- Beginning of the reaction — greatest chance of a collision — maximum number of acid particles and marble chips at their largest giving most surface for the acid particles to collide with — fastest reaction.
- The acid gets used up — reacting — and the marble chips get smaller — reacting — so the chances of collisions decrease and eventually the reaction slows down and gets slower until one of the reactants is completely used up — it stops.
  Effect of changing conditions
- If we do the same experiment as above with different conditions, making sure that it is a fair test, we can compare the effects of different conditions.

CLASSIFYING MATERIALS AND CONSIDERING REACTIONS

> Note – get same amount of product.

- We get this graph if plotted on the same axes:

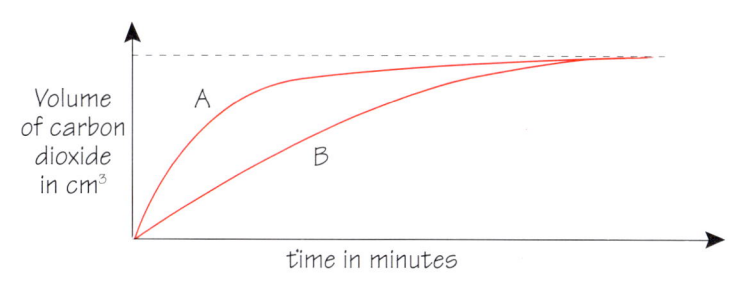

  Graph: Volume of carbon dioxide in cm³ vs time in minutes, showing curve A rising faster than curve B, both reaching the same plateau.

- **Changing temperature** – higher temperature gives faster rate – graph A – reactant particles have more energy – move faster – collide more and with greater energy.
- **Changing concentration** – more concentrated acid gives faster rate – graph A – more reactant particles in a certain volume so more chances of collisions.
- **Changing surface area** – smaller chips (greater surface area) gives faster rate – graph A – collisions happen on surface of solid reactants.
- **Changing gas pressure** – when reactants include gases a higher pressure gives a faster rate – graph A – pressure pushes particles closer so more chance of collision.
- **Using a catalyst** – catalysts can increase rate without being used up themselves – graph A – different reactions need different catalysts – reduce the activation energy, e.g. manganese dioxide catalyses decomposition of hydrogen peroxide.
- Making reactions go faster – increasing the rate – is very important industrially – the faster the product can be made the less costly it will be.

Reversible reactions

- Some reactions can happen in both directions – the products can become the reactants – shown by a double arrow   reactants $\rightleftharpoons$ products
- Sometimes the conditions make the reaction happen one way or another:

  e.g.   ammonium chloride$_{(s)}$ $\underset{cool}{\overset{heat}{\rightleftharpoons}}$ ammonia$_{(g)}$ + hydrogen chloride$_{(g)}$

- Sometimes both reactions happen at once, e.g. the Haber process:

  endothermic – $N_{2(g)} + 3H_{2(g)} \rightleftharpoons 2NH_{3(g)}$ – **exothermic**

- In a closed container both reactions would take place until they were going at the same rate – the proportions of the substances would then not change – **equilibrium**.
- In industry it is vital to get the conditions of the reaction so that the proportion of the desired product in this equilibrium mixture is as high as possible **economically**.

> Equilibrium mixture alters to reduce the effect of the change – Le Chatelier's Principle.

Effect of increasing temperature
speeds up the rate of both reactions
increases products of endothermic reactions
decreases products of exothermic reactions

Effect of decreasing temperature
slows down the rate of both reactions **
increases products of exothermic reactions *
decreases products of endothermic reactions

Reaction which produces ammonia is exothermic (reverse is endothermic)
∴ to increase amount of ammonia at equilibrium should **decrease temperature** *

> Examiners are keen on the idea of why this temperature is used.

But – reactions would come to equilibrium too slowly. **
- **So** – use a compromise temperature of about 450° C.
- In practice the reaction mixture does not get to equilibrium – the mixture from the reaction vessel is continually removed – ammonia is removed by cooling the gases. Ammonia becomes a liquid – separated from the unreacted nitrogen and hydrogen – these gases are put back into the reaction vessel.
- A catalyst of tiny pellets of iron (large surface area) speeds up the reaction.
- The gases are reacted at high pressure (200 atmospheres) – this also pushes the equilibrium towards the ammonia – but high pressure is dangerous and expensive.

47

MATERIALS AND THEIR PROPERTIES

Metals and non-metals

The elements have properties which divides them into two broad sets: most (75%) are **metals** – rest (25%) are **non-metals**.

metals	properties	non-metals
often grey solids (except gold, copper)	**appearance**	easily melted solids, a liquid (Br) or gases
high melting point (except mercury and the alkali metals)	**melting point and boiling points**	low melting and boiling points (except carbon, silicon, germanium)
often shiny when cut	**shininess**	usually dull
more dense	**density**	less dense
tough, strong, can easily be bent or hammered to shape	**toughness**	brittle, easily broken or crumbly
good conductors when solid or liquid	**electrical conduction**	poor conductors (except graphite)
good conductors when solid or liquid	**heat conduction**	poor conductors when solid or liquid
basic – metal oxide or hydroxide reacts with an acid	**acid/base properties of oxide**	acidic – non-metal oxides react with bases
metal atoms try to lose electrons	**structure**	non-metal atoms try to gain electrons

Note that the above are just a guide to the differences, not absolute rules.

Uses of some metals

The uses to which metals are put depend on several things:

- the properties of the particular metal in terms of melting point, conduction etc.
- the reactivity – see p. 49
- how available the metal is and what it costs
- if the metal can be mixed with something else – **alloyed** – to improve its properties.

Uses of aluminium:
- overhead power cables – very good conductor, low density
- aeroplane bodies – strong (especially alloys), low density
- window and door frames – attractive, doesn't corrode (react with air, water)
- kitchen foil – shiny, doesn't corrode, doesn't melt easily, strong in thin sheets
- pots and pans – doesn't corrode with kitchen liquids, not damaged by handling
- some drinks cans – not dense, doesn't corrode, easily shaped, can be recycled.

Uses of iron – mainly when mixed with less than 1% carbon → steel:
- structural beams for buildings and oil rigs – strong, rigid, easy to shape and join by welding and rivetting, available in large amounts at lower cost than other metals
- ships, cars – very strong, joined by rivetting or welding, painted to prevent rust
- tools and machines – can be shaped by casting, hardness improved by tempering.

Uses of copper:
- electrical wiring – very good conductor, can be pulled into wire, bends to shape
- water piping – easily shaped, easily joined, not toxic, doesn't corrode
- coinage – doesn't corrode, alloys to give harder silvery or bronze types.

GCSE Success
with Letts Educational

FREE Revision Planner overleaf

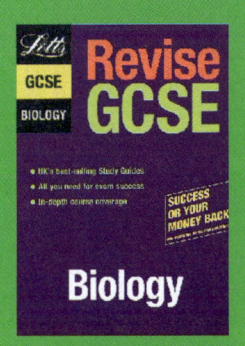

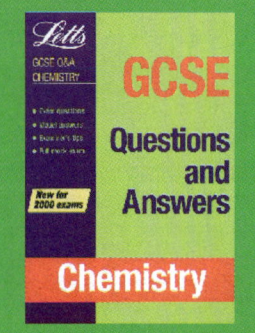

Revise GCSE
The UK's best selling study guides, provide all you need for exam success! Each guide offers complete study and reference support throughout your GCSE Course. We're so sure of this series it even comes with a 'success or your money back' guarantee.

Questions and Answers
Practice, Practice, Practice ... that's the secret to GCSE success. Examiners say that practice really does improve your GCSE grade.

The Letts Question and Answers series provides

- Questions specifically written by examiners for their relevance to the year 2000 exams
- Full Answers to every question with step-by-step explanations
- Examiner's tips to achieve maximum marks and avoid common mistakes

This series is crucial for improving your exam technique and performance

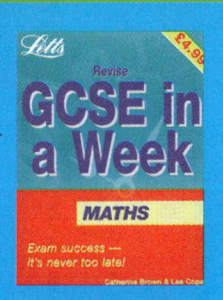

Save £5 when you purchase Revise GCSE and a GCSE Q&A

Revise GCSE in a Week
The ultimate series to help you in the crucial week before your exams begin
DON'T PANIC – in one week or less this book will
- Give you the information that you really need; and no more
- Make sure the essentials really sink in
- Provide a timed revision programme to keep you on course

Created by the staff of one of the UK's most successful tutorial colleges, this one-week crammer course gives you the inside knowledge for GCSE success – the ideal refresher course to reinforce your revision

Save £2 when you purchase a GCSE in a Week and a GCSE Passcards

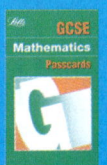

GCSE Passcards
Concise revision notes especially prepared by examiners, giving you security in the knowledge that you are learning the essentials. With a clear Lay-out using summary lists and key points, Passcards are the ideal quick revision tool.

Grade A Secrets
The ultimate mock exams.
GCSE examiners have written these papers in the same style and format as the GCSE exams. Each pack contains
- Examiners report on what 1999 students did wrong and how to get it right
- Examiners analysis of what is likely to come up in this years exams

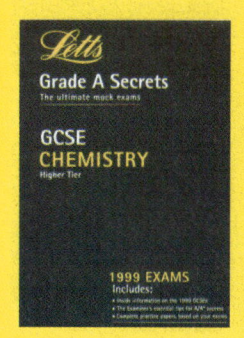

Special Offers – save £££££s

Order any GCSE in a week and Passcards and save £2

Order any Revise GCSE and Questions and Answers and save £5

To order see the back page

Letts GCSE Year Planner

This revision planner is designed for you to pull out and use. It will help you prepare well and organise your revision – as well as boosting your confidence and your grades! Stick the planner on your wall and mark on key dates in your revision programme.

We ha
- Terr
- Mo
- You

Your future starts here

1999

September
Start of your final GCSE Year
Make your life easier – and avoid stress and panic later on – start preparing for your GCSEs NOW!

Letts Revise GCSE has all the crucial content, exam practice and advice that you need to support you throughout your course right up to your exams.

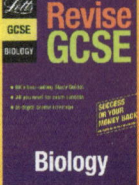

October
Coursework is important
Understand and learn your coursework thoroughly – it can count for 20-60% of your final mark.

The secret of exam success is practice, practice and more practice. *Letts GCSE Q&A* contains specially selected exam questions with answers; examiner's tips and a full mock exam paper.

November
Start revising for mock exams
Take your mock exams seriously – they test your knowledge, and give you important practice in answering exam questions.

December
Mock Exams
Get the most from your mocks. Improve your exam technique:
- read the questions carefully
- underline key words in the questions
- allocate your time according to marks
- answer the question asked!

Letts Grade A Secrets is the ultimate moc Two full length exam papers and mark schem actual exams, while GCSE examiners revea information on how to get A/A* grad

2000

January
Learn from you mocks
Mock exams can he you and your teache assess your progres Use your mock resu check that you have the information and revision aids that yo need for the rest of year.

Day	Sept	Oct	Nov	Dec	Jan
Monday			1		
Tuesday			2		
Wednesday	1		3	1	
Thursday	2		4	2	
Friday	3	1	5	3	
Saturday	4	2	6	4	1
Sunday	5	3	7	5	2
Monday	6	4	8	6	3
Tuesday	7	5	9	7	4
Wednesday	8	6	10	8	5
Thursday	9	7	11	9	6
Friday	10	8	12	10	7
Saturday	11	9	13	11	8
Sunday	12	10	14	12	9
Monday	13	11	15	13	10
Tuesday	14	12	16	14	11
Wednesday	15	13	17	15	12
Thursday	16	14	18	16	13
Friday	17	15	19	17	14
Saturday	18	16	20	18	15
Sunday	19	17	21	19	16
Monday	20	18	22	20	17
Tuesday	21	19	23	21	18
Wednesday	22	20	24	22	19
Thursday	23	21	25	23	20
Friday	24	22	26	24	21
Saturday	25	23	27	25	22
Sunday	26	24	28	26	23
Monday	27	25	29	27	24
Tuesday	28	26	30	28	25
Wednesday	29	27		29	26
Thursday	30	28		30	27
Friday		29		31	28
Saturday		30			29
Sunday		31			30
Monday					31

GCSE Exam

Letts EDUCATIONAL

...ated key dates in the revision calendar, but you might want to mark on:
- ...and holidays
- Coursework deadlines
- ...dates
- An outline revision plan
- ...exam timetable

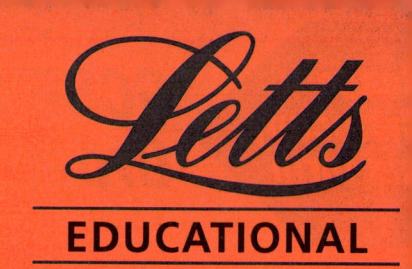

February
...busy – only 4 ...nths to go to ...r GCSEs

...ning your work ...s that you are more ...y to revise properly ...vill also help you ...cool and avoid ...s.

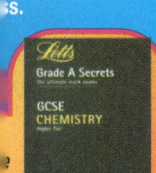

March
Make a plan

Prepare your revision plan. Make sure you fill in all your commitments including:
- lesson times
- school activities
- other activities (part-time jobs etc)
- time for relaxation and enjoyment.

GCSE in a week is a timed revision programme to keep you on course. It will give you the information you really need to learn and no more as well as final important practice.

April
Exam success – it's never too late

Even if you are feeling the strain – don't panic there is still time to brush up on your knowledge and exam technique.

May
One month to go

Like an athlete training for an important event, you should now be reaching your peak. During the weeks before the exams:
- get plenty of rest and sleep
- refresh your memory on the difficult or essential points
- catch up if you are behind – but don't overdo it.

June
Start of GCSEs

Stay calm and don't get stressed out the night before the first exam:
- check your exam timetable and know which room the exam is in and what time it starts
- make sure you have all your equipment
- make sure you know the centre number & your candidate number

July
Congratulations your exams are over!

Good luck!

GCSE Passcards are the perfect last-minute revision aid. These handy cards have all the key information you need to brush up on.

See overleaf for how to order...

Success with Letts

Please photocopy this form

GCSE Revision Order Form

Special offers apply only when ordered directly from the publisher. Private orders to home addresses should include £1.00 postage & packing per book (up to £3.00 i.e. 3 books or more). There are three easy ways to place your order:
1. Telephone us on our FREEPHONE number 0800 216592
2. Fax your order to us on 0208 740 2280
3. Or send your order to our FREEPOST address:
   Letts Educational, FREEPOST, London W12 8BR

Your books should arrive between 5 and 7 working days.

Order any GCSE in a Week and Passcards and save £2

Title	ISBN	Price	Qty	Value
GCSE Revision & Exam Preparation	**1 84085**			
Science Foundation Revision Notes (NEAB)	2887	£3.00		
Science Higher Revision Notes (NEAB)	2879	£3.00		
Biology Revision Notes (gen)	2909	£3.00		
Chemistry Revision Notes (gen)	2895	£3.00		
Physics Revision Notes (gen)	2917	£3.00		
Science Foundation Revision Notes (gen)	2860	£3.00		
Science Higher Revision Notes (gen)	2852	£3.00		
Maths Foundation Revision Notes (gen)	2925	£3.00		
Maths Intermediate Revision Notes (gen)	2933	£3.00		
Maths Higher Revision Notes (gen)	2941	£3.00		
Maths Foundation Revision Notes (Edexcel/London)	295X	£3.00		
Maths Intermediate Revision Notes (Edexcel/London)	2968	£3.00		
Maths Higher Revision Notes (Edexcel/London)	2976	£3.00		
GCSE French Revision Notes (includes audio CD)	2992	£4.00		
GCSE Geography Revision Notes	2984	£3.00		
GCSE Revision Skills Booklet	1449	£1.00		
Improve your GCSE Grades	2143	£1.00		
Letts Revise Guides	**1 85805**			
Biology	4206	£9.99		
Business Studies	4214	£9.99		
Chemistry	4222	£9.99		
Design and Technology	4230	£9.99		
English	4249	£9.99		
English Literature	4257	£9.99		
French (with audio CD)	4265	£13.99		
French (book only)	4273	£9.99		
Geography	4281	£9.99		
German (with audio CD)	429X	£13.99		
German (book only)	4303	£9.99		
History (1750 – present)	4311	£9.99		
Human Biology	432X	£9.99		
Information Technology	4338	£9.99		
Mathematics	4346	£9.99		
Media Studies	4354	£9.99		
Physics	4362	£9.99		
Physical Education	4370	£9.99		
Psychology	4389	£9.99		
Religious Studies	4397	£9.99		
Science	4400	£11.99		
Sociology	4419	£9.99		
Spanish (with audio CD)	4427	£13.99		
Spanish (book only)	4435	£9.99		
World History (1870 – present)	4443	£9.99		

Save £5 when you purchase Revise GCSE and a GCSE Q&A

Sub-total ____
Bulk purchase discount ____
postage ____
Grand Total £ ____

Order any Revise GCSE and Questions and Answers and save £5

Title	ISBN	Price	Qty	Value
GCSE Questions and Answers	**1 85758**			
Biology	9505	£5.99		
Business Studies	9513	£5.99		
Chemistry	9521	£5.99		
English	953X	£5.99		
French (with audio CD)	9548	£8.99		
Geography	9556	£5.99		
German (with audio CD)	9564	£8.99		
Information Technology	9572	£5.99		
Mathematics	9580	£5.99		
Mathematics to A*	9599	£5.99		
Modern World History	9602	£5.99		
Physics	9610	£5.99		
Schools History Project	9629	£5.99		
Science	9637	£7.99		
Spanish (with audio CD)	9645	£8.99		
Revise GCSE in a Week	**1 85758**			
Biology	6956	£4.99		
Business Studies	9459	£4.99		
Chemistry	6964	£4.99		
English	6972	£4.99		
French (with audio CD)	6980	£8.99		
Geography	6999	£4.99		
Maths	7006	£4.99		
Maths to A*	9475	£4.99		
Modern World History	9467	£4.99		
Physics	7014	£4.99		
Science	7022	£6.99		
Letts Essentials for GCSE	**1 84085**			
GCSE Maths Coursework Student's Guide	1651	£1.00		
GCSE Maths for Scientists	1503	£1.00		
GCSE Maths Dictionary	1236	£1.00		
GCSE Science Foundation Coursework Student's Guide	121X	£1.00		
GCSE Science Higher Coursework Student's Guide	1457	£1.00		
GCSE Science Dictionary	1465	£1.00		
GCSE English Spelling & Vocabulary	1392	£2.00		
GCSE English Punctuation & Grammar	1406	£2.00		
GCSE French Vocabulary Book	1414	£2.00		
GCSE French Grammar Guide	0825	£2.00		
GCSE German Vocabulary Book	1422	£2.00		
GCSE Spanish Vocabulary Book	1430	£2.00		
A Level Revision Notes	**1 84085**			
A Level Revision Skills Booklet	0809	£1.00		
A Level Maths Revision Notes	0922	£5.00		
A Level Chemistry Revision Notes	0949	£5.00		
A Level Biology Revision Notes	0965	£5.00		
A Level Physics Revision Notes	0981	£5.00		
A Level Business Studies Revision Notes	1007	£5.00		
A Level Psychology Revision Notes	1023	£5.00		
A Level Sociology Revision Notes	1066	£5.00		
A Level Computing Revision Notes	1082	£5.00		

Save £2 when you purchase a GCSE in a Week and a GCSE Passcards

Sub-total ____
Bulk purchase discount ____
postage ____
Grand Total £ ____

"special offers only available when books are purchased direct from the publisher"

☐ I enclose a cheque made payable to The Book Service Ltd

for £ _____

☐ Please invoice our school

☐ Please charge my MasterCard/Visa/Amex/Switch/Delta

Card number ☐☐☐☐ ☐☐☐☐ ☐☐☐☐ ☐☐☐☐

Issue number (for Switch/Delta) ☐☐   Expiry Date ☐☐

Signature _____

Name _____   Position _____
School _____
Address _____
Postcode _____
Telephone _____
Fax _____
E-mail _____

Every effort was made to ensure that all prices and special offers were correct at the time of going to press. However, Letts reserves the right to change these without prior notice.

Letts EDUCATIONAL
9-15 Aldine Street
London W12 8AW
Tel: 0800 216592   Fax: 0208 740 2280
E-mail: schools@lettsed.co.uk

CLASSIFYING MATERIALS AND CONSIDERING REACTIONS

Reactivity of metals

Learn general reaction – note how reactivity modifies it.

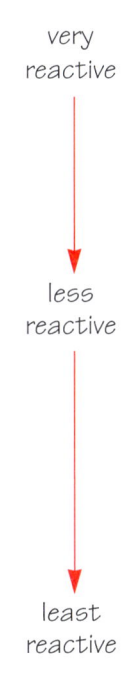

- Metals react similarly but seem to have a different 'enthusiasm' – **reactivity**.
- Can see this by observing how quickly metals react in the same conditions.
- Also see how conditions, e.g. temperature, need to change to get a reaction.
- List in order of reactivity – **reactivity series** – available in Data Book.

very reactive ↓ less reactive ↓ least reactive

	reaction with air	reaction with water	reaction with acid
general reaction	forms metal oxide	forms metal oxide or hydroxide and hydrogen	forms metal salt and hydrogen
potassium	bright lilac flame	quickly in cold water	dangerous to do
sodium	bright yellow flame	quickly in cold water	dangerous to do
calcium	bright red flame	slowly in cold water	dangerous to do
magnesium	bright white flame	only when hot in steam	very fast reaction
aluminium	see below	no reaction	no reaction
carbon			
zinc	slowly – yellow glow	when red hot in steam	reacts steadily
iron	turns slowly black	when red hot in steam	reacts slowly
tin	oxide → on surface	very little reaction	reacts very slowly
lead	oxide → on surface	very little reaction	little reaction
hydrogen			
copper	slowly when heated	no reaction	no reaction
silver	no reaction	no reaction	no reaction
gold	no reaction	no reaction	no reaction
platinum	no reaction	no reaction	no reaction

Use series to predict if a reaction will happen and how quickly.

- Decreasing reactivity from top to bottom.
- Metals stay in this order for all reactions.
- Reactive metals at top – react quickly at low temperatures.
- Less reactive metals in middle – react slowly or need higher temperature to react.
- Non-reactive metals (unreactive) at bottom – don't react at all.

Aluminium often does not react the way its place in the series would suggest – see above:
- because the metal forms a **thin layer of aluminium oxide** on its surface
- this layer stops oxygen, water, acids or other reactants from getting to the metal
- if layer is removed then aluminium reacts according to its place
- layer is sometimes thickened (anodised) to protect the metal.

Elements high in series displace those lower in series from solutions of their salts.

Displacement of metals

- Where a **more reactive** metal takes the place of a **less reactive** metal in a reaction,

  e.g. iron   +   copper II sulphate   →   copper   +   iron II sulphate

  $Fe_{(s)}$ + $CuSO_{4(aq)}$ → $Cu_{(s)}$ + $FeSO_{4(aq)}$

  grey powder   blue solution   pink powder   green solution

Think of it as a competition between metals for something to join up with.

- Iron takes the place of copper – so iron ends up with the sulphate.
- Can use displacement to work out place of a metal in the series.
- Carbon and hydrogen are in the list – not metals but get involved in displacement.
- **Metals above hydrogen will displace it from water and from acids:**

  e.g. calcium + water → calcium hydroxide + hydrogen

  $Ca_{(s)}$ + $2H_2O_{(l)}$ → $Ca(OH)_{2(s)}$ + $H_{2(g)}$

- Carbon will take oxygen (reduce) from metal oxides below it:

  carbon + lead (II) oxide → carbon dioxide + lead

  $C_{(s)}$ + $2PbO_{(s)}$ → $CO_{2(g)}$ + $2Pb_{(l)}$

MATERIALS AND THEIR PROPERTIES

Acids and alkalis

- When substances dissolve in water, the solution behaves in one of three ways.
- These solutions are said to be either **acidic**, **alkaline** or **neutral**.

Acids

- Common laboratory acids – sulphuric (H_2SO_4), hydrochloric (HCl), nitric (HNO_3).
- Sometimes corrosive – dangerous to skin and eyes – solution tastes sour (careful – don't try it).
- Often corrosive to metals – sometimes producing hydrogen,

    e.g.   iron + sulphuric acid → iron II sulphate + hydrogen

    $Fe_{(s)} + H_2SO_{4(aq)} \rightarrow FeSO_{4(aq)} + H_{2(g)}$

- React with metal carbonates by fizzing and giving off carbon dioxide,

    e.g.   calcium carbonate + hydrochloric acid → calcium chloride + carbon dioxide + water

    $CaCO_{3(s)} + 2HCl_{(aq)} \rightarrow CaCl_{2(aq)} + CO_{2(g)} + H_2O_{(l)}$

- Acids are formed when non-metal oxides (compounds of non-metals with oxygen formed often by burning the non-metal) dissolve in water:

    e.g. sulphur dioxide SO_2, carbon dioxide CO_2 and nitrogen dioxide NO_2

    sulphur dioxide + water → sulphurous acid (cause of acid rain)

    $SO_{2(g)} + H_2O_{(l)} \rightarrow H_2SO_{3(aq)}$

- Compounds of hydrogen and a halogen (hydrogen halides) produce acid solutions,

    e.g. hydrogen iodide$_{(g)}$ + water$_{(l)}$ → hydroiodic acid$_{(aq)}$

    hydrogen chloride → hydrochloric acid

    hydrogen bromide → hydrobromic acid.

Alkalis

- Alkalis are formed when some metal oxides (compounds of metals with oxygen formed often by burning the metal) or metal hydroxides dissolve in water,

    e.g. sodium, potassium and calcium oxides and hydroxide (others don't dissolve)

    calcium oxide + water → calcium hydroxide (limewater)

    $CaO_{(s)} + H_2O_{(l)} \rightarrow Ca(OH)_{2(aq)}$

- Alkalis react with acids giving a salt and water only,

    e.g.   **alkali**   **acid**   **salt**

    sodium hydroxide + hydrochloric acid → sodium chloride + water

    $NaOH_{(aq)} + HCl_{(aq)} \rightarrow NaCl_{(aq)} + H_2O_{(l)}$

- Some are quite corrosive (caustic) also – dangerous to skin and especially eyes.

Neutral solutions

Remember litmus colours

acid	alkali
red	blue

- Water is a neutral substance – it is not acid or alkali.
- Most substances which dissolve do not form acids or alkalis – they are neutral.

Indicators – acids and alkalis change the colour of substances called indicators.

Strength of acids and alkalis

- Some solutions behave like weak acids – they don't do acid things very well.
- Some solutions behave like strong acids – they do all acid things very well.
- Alkalis also can be weak or strong.
- Strength is not the same as concentration – how much water is in the solution.
- To measure the strength of acids and alkalis – find their **pH value on the pH scale**.

CLASSIFYING MATERIALS AND CONSIDERING REACTIONS

pH scale

```
0  1  2  3  4  5  6  7  8  9  10  11  12  13  14
very strong  strong      weak   neutral   weak      strong   very strong
    ←        increasing acidity  ————————  increasing alkalinity  →
```

- pH < 7 – acid, pH = 7 – neutral, pH > 7 – alkali.
- To find the pH value for a solution:
  - can use a pH meter – dip the probe in the solution – read the value on the meter
  - add a few drops of Universal Indicator to the solution – this goes a whole range of colours depending on the pH of the solution – see Data Book for colours.

Neutralisation

- Acids and alkalis are like chemical opposites – they can cancel each other out – this is called **neutralisation** – because it causes neutral substances to form.
- Neutralisation is a particular chemical reaction
  acid + alkali → salt + water.
- Any acid and any alkali can neutralise each other – they produce different **salts**.
- Common salt, table salt – sodium chloride, is only one example of a salt.
- The salt produced depends on the **metal** – from the alkali and the **particular acid** used,

  e.g. sulphuric acid   → salts called metal sulphates
        nitric acid   → salts called metal nitrates
        hydrochloric acid → salts called metal chlorides,

  e.g. sulphuric acid + sodium hydroxide → sodium sulphate + water
        $H_2SO_{4(aq)}$ + $2NaOH_{(aq)}$ → $Na_2SO_{4(aq)}$ + $2H_2O_{(l)}$

Practise working out the salt from different acids and alkalis.

The ammonium ion NH_4^+ forms salts like a metal.

Some useful salts

- **Sodium chloride** – contains the alkali metal, sodium and the halogen, chlorine.
- These are present as positive sodium ions (Na^+) and negative chloride ions (Cl^-).
- It occurs naturally dissolved in sea water and also in large underground deposits formed when prehistoric seas dried up and became buried.
- It is dug up and used in large amounts to spread on roads to stop ice forming.
- It is purified and used in food preparation and flavouring.
- It is also the raw material in the chlor–alkali chemical industry.

The chlor–alkali process

- This involves the electrolysis of sodium chloride solution (known as brine).
- Water is pumped underground to dissolve the salt and the brine is pumped out.
- The brine is put in a special container – called a cell – and electrolysis takes place.
- At the **positive** electrode, negative chloride ions become **chlorine** gas,
  $2Cl^-_{(aq)} - 2e^- → Cl_{2(g)}$
- At the **negative** electrode, positive hydrogen ions become hydrogen,
  $2H^+_{(aq)} + 2e^- → H_{2(g)}$
- The solution also changes and becomes sodium hydroxide.
- The three products are very useful in a variety of ways.

product	chlorine	hydrogen	sodium hydroxide
uses of each substance	in water treatment – to kill bacteria / in swimming pools – to kill bacteria / to manufacture disinfectants and bleaches / to manufacture P.V.C. – a plastic	to manufacture ammonia – see section on air / to react with edible oils to make margarine	to manufacture soap, paper and ceramics

Silver halides – these are salts of the metal silver and a halogen.
silver chloride (AgCl), silver bromide (AgBr), silver iodide (AgI):
- used to make photographic films and photographic paper
- light or x rays or radiation makes the compounds decompose to give silver
- the amount of silver depends on the amount of light which hits the film – so an image is formed – this is made permanent by other chemicals – developing.

51

MATERIALS AND THEIR PROPERTIES

Classifying materials and considering reactions

Questions

1. The process of gases spreading out and mixing is _____
2. Change from liquid to gas is _____ (fast) or _____ (slow)
3. What are the particles in $^{24}_{12}Mg$ _____
4. What are isotopes? _____
5. What ions are formed by $_{13}Al$ _____ $_{20}Ca$ _____ $_{16}S$ _____ $_{9}F$ _____
6. Formula of compound of: Ca and O _____ , Mg and Cl _____
7. Draw a dot and cross diagram of H_2O (in the margin)
8. Why do polymers have a higher m.pt? _____
9. Substances with a giant atomic lattic structure have a high m.pt. Why?
   _____
10. What feature of metal structures allows conduction? _____
11. What does OILRIG mean? _____
12. Reaction at positive electrode in copper purification _____
13. Write and balance the formula equations:
    (a) sodium + oxygen → sodium oxide _____
    (b) hydrogen + oxygen → water _____
    (c) magnesium + aluminium oxide → magnesium oxide + aluminium
    _____
14. Equations for electrolysis of aluminium oxide _____
    _____
15. In the diagram what does A) _____ and
    B) _____ show.
16. Draw an energy level diagram (in the margin) for carbon burning with oxygen.
17. Complete this. Rate of reaction depends on how frequently reactant particles _____ . The energy of these must be greater than the _____ energy to make them react.
18. Why does surface area affect the rate of reaction between a solid and a liquid?
    _____
19. Why does a catalyst affect the rate of a chemical reaction ? _____
    _____
20. Haber process. Catalyst _____ temperature _____ pressure _____
21. What happens at equilibrium? _____
22. Metals atoms try to _____ electrons and metal oxides are _____ .
23. Give two uses of copper _____ _____
24. Why does aluminium appear to be less reactive than it actually is?
    _____
25. Does hydrogen react with copper (II) oxide ? _____ Why (or why not)
    _____ Products _____
26. Zinc + hydrochloric acid → _____ + _____
27. Calcium hydroxide + nitric acid → _____ + _____
28. Liquid product from electrolysis of brine? _____

PATTERNS OF BEHAVIOUR AND USING RAW MATERIALS

Patterns of behaviour and using raw materials
The Periodic Table

- Elements were discovered gradually as scientists explored different substances.
- 18th– 20th century scientists looked for patterns in properties of elements.
- Dobereiner – found sets of three elements (triads) – middle one behaved like the average of the other two, e.g. chlorine, bromine, iodine.
- Newlands – put elements in order of atomic mass – sometimes (not always) noted similar properties every eight elements – called it Law of Octaves.
- Mendeleev – also put elements in order of atomic mass – arranged in rows under each other so elements with similar properties ended up in columns – left blanks for elements still to be discovered – used the pattern to predict the properties of these – he was right – pattern is very similar to modern complete Periodic Table.

Modern Periodic Table (see Periodic Table in Data Book)

- Elements arranged in order of proton number (atomic number) – no gaps now.
- Pattern is of horizontal rows – various lengths – called **periods**.
- Pattern also has vertical columns – elements with similar properties – **groups**.

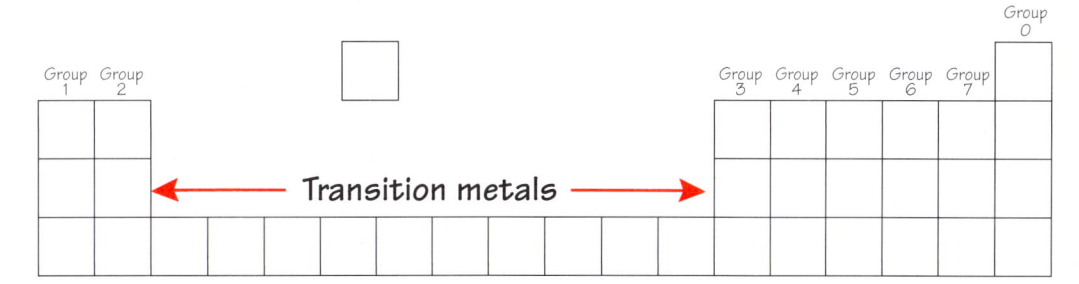

What causes the pattern of the Periodic Table?

- Pattern of Periodic Table results from the electron arrangements of atoms.
- The proton number is the number of protons each element has – same as the number of electrons.
- As number of electrons increases by one – electron arrangement changes.

Hydrogen is not actually in group 1. Shown here to fit in with pattern of electron arrangement.

The electron arrangement for the first twenty elements – make sure you see how it makes the pattern of the table.

GP1	GP2	GP3	GP4	GP5	GP6	GP7	GP0	
H 1							He 2	1st period (1st shell filling)
Li 2,1	Be 2,2	B 2,3	C 2,4	N 2,5	O 2,6	F 2,7	Ne 2,8	2nd period (2nd shell filling)
Na 2,8,1	Mg 2,8,2	Al 2,8,3	Si 2,8,4	P 2,8,5	S 2,8,6	Cl 2,8,7	Ar 2,8,8	3rd period (3rd shell filling)

- Beginning of each period – new energy level – only one electron in outer level – elements in this column (**group 1**) behave similarly (**alkali metals**).
- End of each period – energy level full – elements in this column (**group 0**) behave similarly (**noble gases**).
- Elements just before end of each period – nearly full energy level – seven electrons in outer level – elements in this column (**group 7**) behave similarly (**halogens**).
- Elements on the left of the table – energy levels starting to fill – lose electrons to get stable – form positive ions – **metals**.
- Elements on the right of table – energy levels nearly full – gain electrons to get stable – form negative ions – **non-metals**.

53

MATERIALS AND THEIR PROPERTIES

Transition metals

- Not easy to explain how this block of metals fits into the pattern.
- Some very important and useful metals in this block, e.g. iron, copper.
- Have similar properties
  – form coloured compounds, e.g. blue copper sulphate
  – have high melting points.
- Can often be used as catalysts; iron – in making ammonia – Haber process; platinum – oxidation of ammonia; nickel – reaction of hydrogen with unsaturated organic compounds – in making margarine.

Alkali metals

Group one (1) (lithium, sodium, potassium, rubidium, caesium, francium)
- Soft (easily cut) grey metals – kept in oil to prevent reaction with air or water.
- Show shiny silvery surface after cutting – quickly tarnishes as reacts with oxygen.
- Burn in air with coloured flame – lithium (red) – sodium (yellow) – potassium (lilac):
  e.g. sodium + oxygen → sodium oxide
       $4Na + O_2 \rightarrow 2Na_2O$
- Melting and boiling point – low for metals – get lower as go down group.
- Form positive ions with a single charge by losing the electron from the outer level,
  e.g. $Na (2,8,1) - e^- \rightarrow Na^+(2,8)$
- Form ionic compounds with negatively charged ions,
  e.g. $2Na_{(l)} + Cl_{2(g)} \rightarrow 2Na^+Cl^-_{(s)}$
- React with water → hydrogen gas and soluble metal hydroxides,
  e.g. lithium + water → hydrogen + lithium hydroxide
       $2Li_{(s)} + 2H_2O_{(l)} \rightarrow H_{2(g)} + 2LiOH_{(aq)}$

These are alkalis – hence name.

Reactivity of the alkali metals:
- metals are reactive (react enthusiastically) and get **more** reactive down the group
- reactivity shows in reaction with oxygen, other non-metals and with water.

Alkali metals with cold water – similar to above – differences due to reactivity:
- lithium stays solid – bubbles rapidly – gradually gets smaller as it reacts
- sodium melts to a ball – fizzes very rapidly on surface – quickly gets smaller
- potassium melts – bubbles catch fire – metal ball sometimes explodes.

What causes the trend in reactivity of the alkali metals?
- All have **one electron** in the highest occupied energy level (outer shell) – group one.
- When they react they lose this electron and form a positive ion,
  e.g. $Li - e^- \rightarrow Li^+$ (oxidation – electron loss).
- Alkali metal atoms get bigger down the group – more electrons – more shells,
  e.g. Li (2,1)   Na (2,8,1)   K (2,8,8,1).
- As the atoms get bigger the electron in the outer shell is more easily lost because
  – it is further from the attraction of the nucleus
  – there are more full shells of electrons to shield the outer electron from the pull of the nucleus.
- The more easily it is lost, the more reactive the atom will be.
- Alkali metals get more reactive the further down the group they are.

Reactivity increases down group from Li to Cs.

PATTERNS OF BEHAVIOUR AND USING RAW MATERIALS

Halogens

Group seven (7) (**fluorine, chlorine, bromine, iodine, astatine**)
- Reactive non-metals — elements are corrosive and toxic.
- Physical properties gradually change down group — melting and boiling points increase — so different states at room temp — colour gets darker.

Learn colours and state – do not try to learn m.pt etc. – just notice the trend.

F_2	colourless gas	m.pt	−220 °C	b.pt	−188 °C	
Cl_2	pale green gas	m.pt	−101 °C	b.pt	−35 °C	
Br_2	red brown liquid	m.pt	−7 °C	b.pt	59 °C	– forms brown vapour
I_2	black solid	m.pt	114 °C	b.pt	184 °C	– forms purple vapour

- Form ionic compounds with metals — gain electrons to form ions with single negative charge; chloride Cl^-, bromide Br^-, iodide I^-, called halide ions.
- Form covalent compounds with non-metals
- Two atoms of each halogen join naturally together to form molecule (**diatomic**) — F_2, Cl_2, Br_2, I_2.

Reactivity of the halogens

- The halogens get **less** reactive down the group.
- Reactivity shows in reaction with metals, hydrogen and in displacement reactions,
  e.g. **chlorine** $_{(g)}$ + **sodium bromide** $_{(aq)}$ → **bromine** $_{(l)}$ + **sodium chloride** $_{(aq)}$
  $Cl_{2(g)}$ + $2NaBr_{(aq)}$ → $Br_{2(l)}$ + $2NaCl_{(aq)}$

Displacement reactions — similar to displacement of metals:

	sodium fluoride	sodium chloride	**sodium bromide**	sodium iodide
fluorine	no reaction	get Cl_2 –smell	get Br_2 – brown	get I_2 – black
chlorine	no reaction	no reaction	**get Br_2 – brown**	get I_2 – black
bromine	no reaction	no reaction	no reaction	I_2 – black
iodine	no reaction	no reaction	no reaction	no reaction

What causes the trend in reactivity of the halogens?
- They all have seven electrons in the highest occupied energy level (outer shell).
- They all try to gain one more electron when they react — form negative ion, e.g. $Cl + e^- \rightarrow Cl^-$.
- The atoms get bigger the further down the group they are — more electron shells.
- The bigger atoms find it harder to attract the extra electron — because
  – it is further from the attraction of the nucleus
  – there are more full electron shells shielding the attraction of the nucleus.
- So the halogens get **less reactive** the further **down the group** they are.

reactivity decreases down group from F to I

Displacement reactions in terms of electrons,
  e.g. $Cl_2 + 2NaBr \rightarrow 2NaCl + Br_2$
    In terms of the ions and atoms which change
    $Cl_2 + 2Br^- \rightarrow 2Cl^- + Br_2$ (the sodium ions do not change)
    This shows that the chlorine is taking electrons from the bromide ions
    $Cl_2 + 2e^- \rightarrow 2Cl^-$ this is reduction — the chlorine is reduced (RIG)
    $2Br^- - 2e^- \rightarrow Br_2$ this is oxidation — the bromide ions are oxidised (OIL)
- Displacement reactions are **redox** reactions.

55

MATERIALS AND THEIR PROPERTIES

Noble gases

Group zero (0) (**helium, neon, argon, krypton, xenon, radon**)
- Very unreactive gases – exist as single atoms – **monatomic**
  – unreactive because they all have a full outer shell of electrons
  – this is a very stable structure – they do not want to gain or lose electrons.
- Air contains about 1% argon and tiny amounts of the others.
- Unreactivity makes them useful:
  – argon to fill light bulbs – stops filament vaporising
  – helium to fill balloons and airships – won't catch fire like hydrogen would
  – neon in a tube glows when electric spark passes through it – signs and displays.

Hydrogen

Not put in a group – it can lose its electron like a metal or gain one like a non-metal.

Useful products from the air

- **Nitrogen** – 79% of the air – is fairly unreactive.
- Plant roots need to take in **soluble nitrogen compounds** from soil to grow well.
- Lightning and some bacteria naturally put soluble nitrogen compounds into soil.
- World population – need more food – farmers add nitrogen compounds – **fertilisers**.

Manufacture of nitrogen based fertilisers

E.g. ammonium nitrate

Three stages
- nitrogen in air used to make ammonia
- ammonia used to make nitric acid
- ammonia and nitric acid reacted to make ammonium nitrate.

Manufacture of ammonia – by the Haber process

Raw materials – air and natural gas.
- **Air** is liquefied – fractionally distilled – nitrogen is separated.
- **Natural gas** – mainly methane – reacted with steam – produces hydrogen
- **Nitrogen** and **hydrogen** (1:3) are mixed and reacted

  nitrogen + hydrogen $\rightleftharpoons$ ammonia

  $N_{2(g)} + 3H_{2(g)} \rightleftharpoons 2NH_{3(g)}$

- Particular conditions are needed for this reaction to take place economically.
- **Hot** (450 °C) gases under **pressure** (200 at.) react over **iron pellets** – **catalyst**.
- Not all reactants turn to ammonia – get mixture of nitrogen, hydrogen, ammonia.
- Mixture is cooled – ammonia turns to liquid – nitrogen and hydrogen gas recycled.

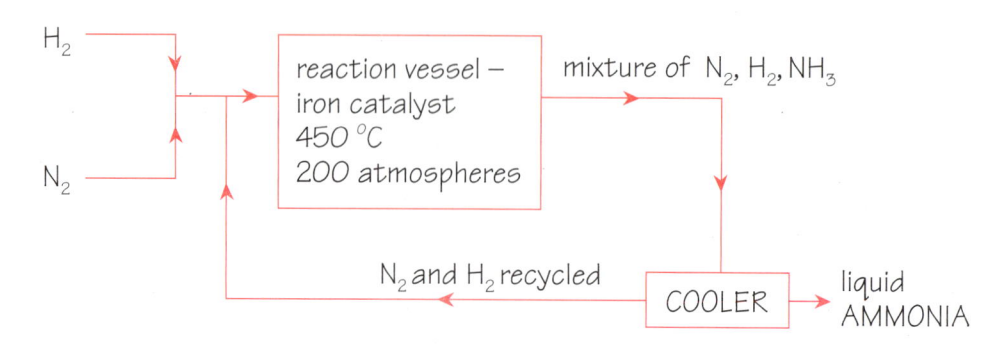

For detail on why these conditions are used see the sections on Energy transfer and Reversible reactions.

H_2 and N_2 → reaction vessel – iron catalyst 450 °C 200 atmospheres → mixture of N_2, H_2, NH_3 → COOLER → liquid AMMONIA; N_2 and H_2 recycled

PATTERNS OF BEHAVIOUR AND USING RAW MATERIALS

Manufacture of nitric acid

- Ammonia is heated with oxygen (oxidation) – exothermic – gives out heat:
  ammonia $_{(g)}$ + oxygen $_{(g)}$ → nitrogen (II) oxide $_{(g)}$ + water $_{(g)}$
- Needs reactant gases at a high temperature (900 °C) passed over a platinum gauze catalyst.
- Nitrogen (II) oxide is cooled – reacted with more oxygen and water → nitric acid:
  nitrogen oxide $_{(g)}$ + oxygen $_{(g)}$ + water $_{(l)}$ → nitric acid $_{(aq)}$

Manufacture of ammonium nitrate – other ammonium salts need other acids

- Nitric acid and ammonia (a base) – react by neutralisation:
  nitric acid $_{(aq)}$ + ammonia $_{(g)}$ → ammonium nitrate $_{(aq)}$
  $HNO_{3(aq)}$ + $NH_{3(g)}$ → $NH_4NO_{3(aq)}$
- The solution of ammonium nitrate is evaporated to give the solid compound.

Advantages of using artificial nitrogen fertilisers:

- nitrogen fertilisers give better yields of crops
- cleaner and simpler to use than natural fertilisers, e.g. manure
- means that fields can be used each year for crops which require nitrogen.

Problems with using nitrates as fertilisers:

- ammonium nitrate is slightly acidic – soil becomes acid
- damage to soil structure from continued use – no humus – old plant material
- they are easily soluble – dissolve in rain and wash out of soil into streams
- promote growth of river weeds – block up river
- slow water – stop oxygen dissolving – weeds rot – rivers become foul
- if river water used for water supply – nitrates very harmful – difficult to remove – possibly cause cancer and blue baby syndrome.

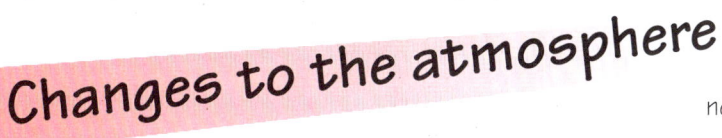

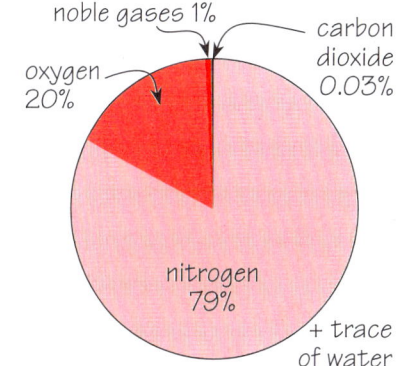

Changes to the atmosphere

noble gases 1%
carbon dioxide 0.03%
oxygen 20%
nitrogen 79%
+ trace of water

- The atmosphere is a mixture of different gases.
- Unusually for a mixture the proportions of the gases are fairly constant.
- This composition has existed for about 200 million years – see below.

Effects of burning – natural and from human activity.

- Burning (or combustion) – when a substance reacts with oxygen – often see flame.
- Produces oxides (compounds with oxygen) – energy released – heat, light,
  e.g. hydrogen $_{(g)}$ + oxygen $_{(g)}$ → water $_{(g)}$ (exothermic reaction).

MATERIALS AND THEIR PROPERTIES

Fuels – particularly fossil fuels burned by industrialised nations.
- **Substances which we burn to give convenient heat**.
- Use different fuels for different uses – see chemicals from oil.
- Often compounds containing **carbon** and **hydrogen** – hydrocarbons.
- Burn to produce **oxides which are gases** – carbon dioxide and water vapour,
  e.g. octane $_{(l)}$ + oxygen $_{(g)}$ → **carbon dioxide** $_{(g)}$ + water $_{(g)}$
- Sometimes fuels (e.g. coal) contains impurities such as **sulphur** – this also burns,
  sulphur $_{(s)}$ + oxygen $_{(g)}$ → **sulphur dioxide** $_{(g)}$
- Fuels burning produce very high temperature, e.g. in a car engine – this can cause the nitrogen and oxygen in the air to combine → **nitrogen oxide.**
- Increasing human population burns more fuels for heat, transport and industry.

Problems caused by burning fuels – **greenhouse effect** – **global warming.**

Greenhouse effect.
- Probably caused by increasing percentage of carbon dioxide in air by burning fuels.
- Natural processes which remove carbon dioxide from air unable to prevent increase
  – photosynthesis reduced by deforestation
  – increased absorption by sea water to form insoluble carbonate sediments and soluble hydrogen carbonates does not compensate for the increase.
- Carbon dioxide in air
  – acts like glass of a greenhouse
  – lets more heat in than out.
- Earth absorbs heat from sun – atmospheric carbon dioxide reduces the amount of heat getting back out.
- Average Earth's temperature gradually increases
  – global warming.
- Leads to climate changes – wet places become dry
  – more and fiercer storms.
- Polar ice caps reduce – more water – sea levels rise – coastal flooding.

Acid rain.
- Sulphur dioxide (and also nitrogen oxide) gases released by burning fuels.
- Gases dissolve in water → acidic solution.
- Rain near areas which burn fuels is acidic – acid rain.
- But also industrial areas can produce gases which wind moves to other places.
- Causes damage to plants – affects leaves – damages soil and roots – trees die.
- Kills river and lake life – after rain the acid level rises in rivers – some lakes have powdered limestone put in them to neutralise some of the acid.
- Metals on buildings react with the acid – discoloured and weakened by corrosion.
- Stonework on buildings is dissolved by acid – weakened and defaced.

Where did the Earth's atmosphere come from?

In the first billion years of the Earth's existence there were constant widespead volcanic eruptions which produced gases as well as the rocks of the Earth's crust.
- This original atmosphere consisted of mainly carbon dioxide – like Venus and Mars.
- Also lots of water vapour and smaller amounts of ammonia and methane.
- As the Earth cooled the water vapour mainly condensed to form the oceans.
- Plant life evolved in the oceans and on the Earth's surface.
- The plants took in carbon dioxide and produced oxygen – photosynthesis.
- As plants, including trees, died, their remains containing the trapped carbon formed huge layers which eventually became coal.
- Carbon dioxide also removed by its reaction with dissolved substances in sea water forming insoluble metal carbonates – these formed sedimentary rocks.
- So carbon dioxide decreased and oxygen increased.

PATTERNS OF BEHAVIOUR AND USING RAW MATERIALS

- Some organisms which thrived in carbon dioxide had fewer places to survive.
- Oxygen in the air reacted with methane and ammonia – releasing nitrogen.
- Nitrogen also released by denitrifying bacteria from materials on the surface.
- Oxygen in the upper atmosphere formed ozone (O_3) – ozone forms a layer which acts as a filter to the ultra-violet (U.V.) radiation which the sun produces.
- With very harmful U.V. radiation reduced – higher organisms like us could evolve.

Structure of the Earth

- Earth shaped like a ball (sphere) – slightly flatter at poles.
- Has layers from surface to centre
  - **crust** – solid rock at surface
  - **mantle** – very thick (viscous) molten rock (magma)
  - **outer core** – molten iron and nickel
  - **inner core** – solid iron and nickel.
- Crust is thicker where continents are, thinner under oceans.
- Crust density is less than average density for Earth – core is more dense.
- Crust made up from three kinds of rock – **igneous**, **sedimentary**, **metamorphic**.

Igneous rocks

- Formed when magma cools and solidifies, e.g. original Earth's crust, volcanic lava.
- Contains randomly arranged interlocking crystals.
- If magma escapes to surface – cools quickly – small dark crystals, e.g. basalt.
- If magma cools inside crust – cools slowly – larger paler crystals, e.g. granite.

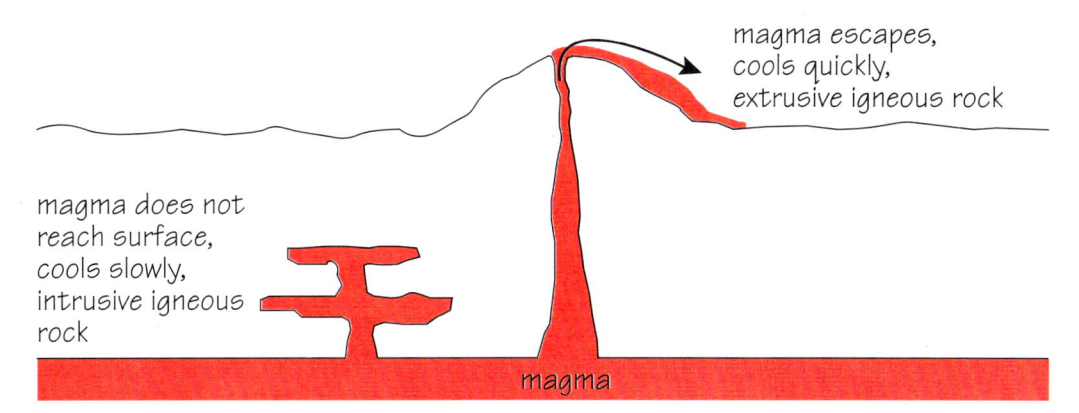

Sedimentary rocks

- Any rocks once formed are subject to weathering and erosion.
- **Weathering** – breakdown of rock by water, ice, wind, plant roots into smaller bits.
- **Erosion** – rocks are carried away by water, gravity – collisions break rock up more.

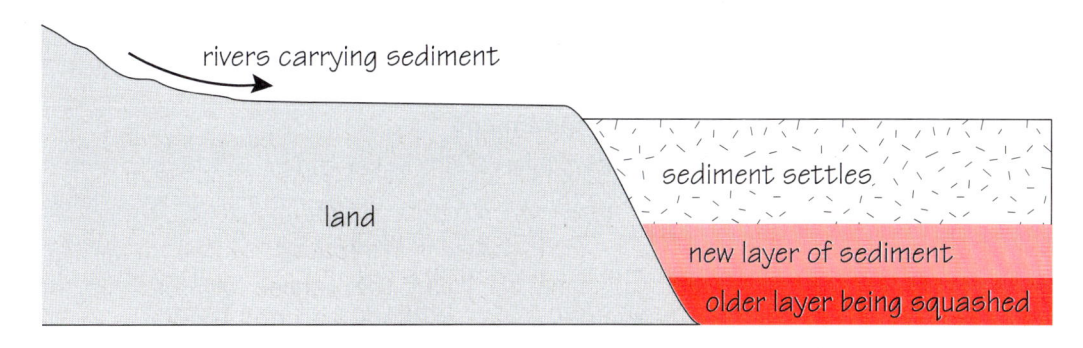

MATERIALS AND THEIR PROPERTIES

- Small bits of rock are called sediment – different sizes and substances.
- Carried towards sea and deposited when water slows down.
- Layer of sediment builds up and weight above squeezes water out of lower layer.
- Dissolved substances – left as water evaporates – act as glue between grains.
- Long time – forms sedimentary rocks, e.g. sand → sandstone, shells → limestone.
- Sedimentary rocks form on top of rocks already there – lower layer must be older.

Fossils

- Bits of plants or animals – trapped in sediment – turn to stone over long period.
- Only in sedimentary rocks – other rock types involve high temperatures – burn up.
- Gives clue about age of rock – if time of existence of plant or animal is known.
- Rocks from different places – containing similar fossils – must be same age.
- Fossils in sedimentary layers – lower layer fossils must be older.

youngest layer with youngest fossils

between layer

oldest layer with oldest fossils

Examiners keen on layers.

Tectonic activity

- Earth's crust is cracked into a number of large pieces – **tectonic plates**.
- Originally all joined in one – shapes of continents show where they used to fit together.
- E. coast of S. America and W. coast of Africa – also rocks and fossils similar.

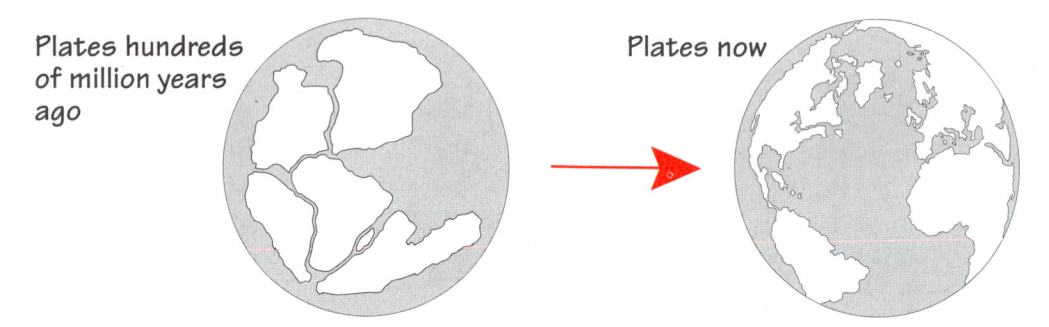

Plates hundreds of million years ago → **Plates now**

- Plates moved and still move because of **convection currents** – radioactive processes inside earth – heat produced – magma moves – moves plates a few cm/year.

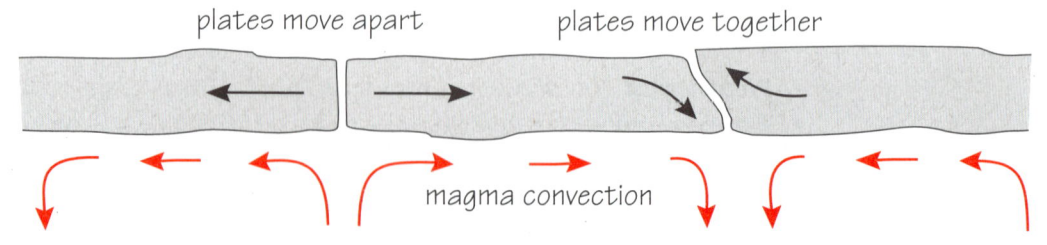

plates move apart   plates move together

magma convection

Evidence for plate movement
Plates move apart – mid ocean ridges on the sea bed – formed as magma escapes:
- magma cools to form new ocean crust – mainly of rock called basalt – rich in iron
- the iron in the basalt becomes magnetised by Earth's magnetic field
- the iron atoms are fixed as the basalt cools and so show the direction of the Earth's magnetism at the time the rock was formed
- if the crust on either side of a mid ocean ridge is examined for magnetism it shows

PATTERNS OF BEHAVIOUR AND USING RAW MATERIALS

clear pattern — symmetrical on each side because crust forms at the ridge and then moves apart with the plates
— periodic reversals of magnetism in the rocks — this matches the reversals in the Earth's magnetism
- mid-Atlantic ridge is a good example of this (see Data Book).

Plates scraping past each other — earthquakes — sudden movement, e.g. Californian coast — get 'fault line' with ground moving in opposite directions.

Plates pushing together
- Sudden movement as one pushes under another — earthquakes.
- More volcanoes around edges of plates — 'ring of fire' around Pacific plate.
- Thinner, denser, oceanic plate is pushed under less dense, thicker, continental plate — subducted (pushed down) plate eventually melts — magma escapes as volcanoes.
- Continental plate is forced upwards — forms mountain ranges over millions of years, e.g. Andes mountain range along the west coast of South America.
- **Metamorphic rocks** — rocks from surface get buried again — as above — intense heat and pressure change rocks — become harder, grains and crystals get smaller — interlock e.g. limestone → marble, mudstone → slate. Often banded, e.g. schist.
- Mountains contain folded, tilted and even upside down sedimentary layers — these must have been formed flat — evidence of unstable crust subject to large forces.

Earlier theory — Earth's surface features due to the crust shrinking and wrinkling as it cooled — now disproved by above evidence.

Rock cycle
- Over millions of years rock types can change from one to another.

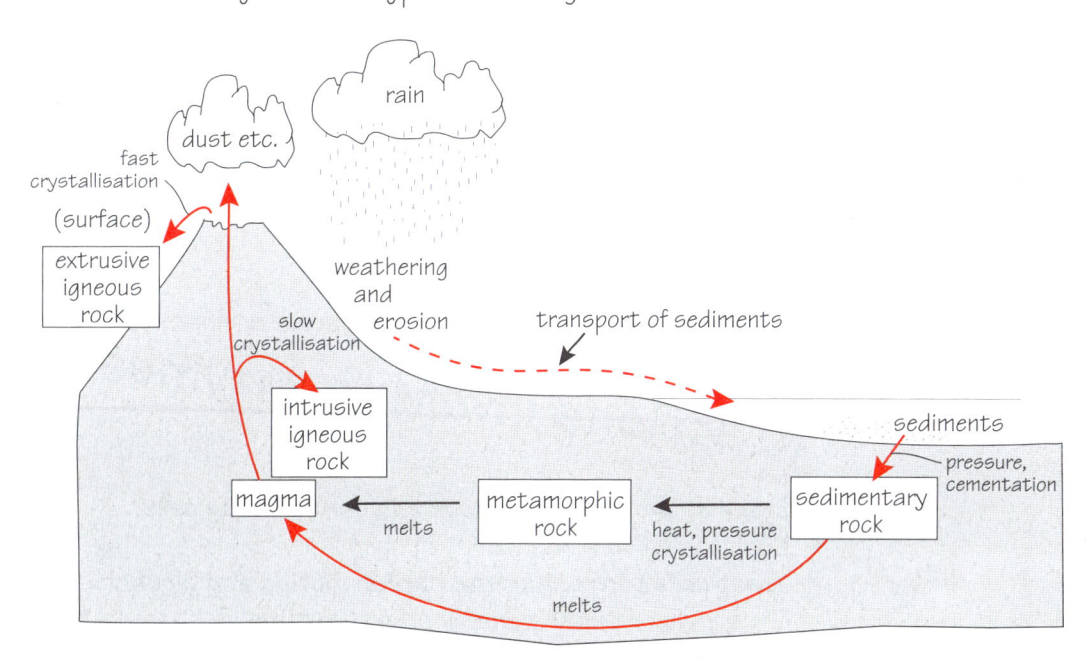

Summary of rock types and their features

Type	Igneous	Sedimentary	Metamorphic
Fine structure	visible interlocking crystals	grains of sediment stuck together	very tiny interlocking crystals
Hardness	quite hard	less hard	very hard
Other features	two types: extrusive/intrusive	often contains fossils	often banded
Examples	basalt, granite	sandstone	gneiss

MATERIALS AND THEIR PROPERTIES

Limestone

- Limestone is a sedimentary rock – formed from shell remains of sea creatures.
- Chalk is a softer rock, marble is a harder metamorphic rock.
- They are all mainly calcium carbonate (Ca CO$_3$).
- Limestone exists in very large quantities – entire hills and ranges – Yorkshire Dales.
- A very useful raw material – extracted in large quantities – by quarrying – a large surface hole – rock loosened by drilling and explosives – moved by large diggers.

Uses of limestone

- As **building stone** – can be shaped into blocks, pillars, window frames, etc. – attacked by acid rain – see reaction below.
- To **neutralise acids in soil and lakes** (caused by acid rain) – powdered and spread
  calcium carbonate + sulphuric acid → calcium sulphate + water + carbon dioxide
  $$Ca CO_{3(s)} + H_2SO_{4(aq)} \rightarrow CaSO_{4(aq)} + H_2O_{(l)} + CO_{2(g)}$$
- To make **calcium oxide** (**quicklime**) and **calcium hydroxide** (**slaked lime**)
  calcium carbonate → heated – furnace (lime kiln) → calcium oxide + carbon dioxide
  $$CaCO_{3(s)} \rightarrow CaO_{(s)} + CO_{2(g)}$$
  calcium oxide + water → calcium hydroxide (heat given out)
  $$CaO_{(s)} + H_2O_{(l)} \rightarrow Ca(OH)_{2(s)}$$

- **Calcium hydroxide** is used to **reduce the acidity of some soils**.
- To make **cement** by roasting powdered limestone and powdered clay in a rotary kiln – cement mixed with water, sand and crushed rock (gravel) makes **concrete** – sets quickly – gradually hardens over time – hard stone for building – widely used.
- To make **glass** by heating limestone, sand and sodium carbonate (soda).

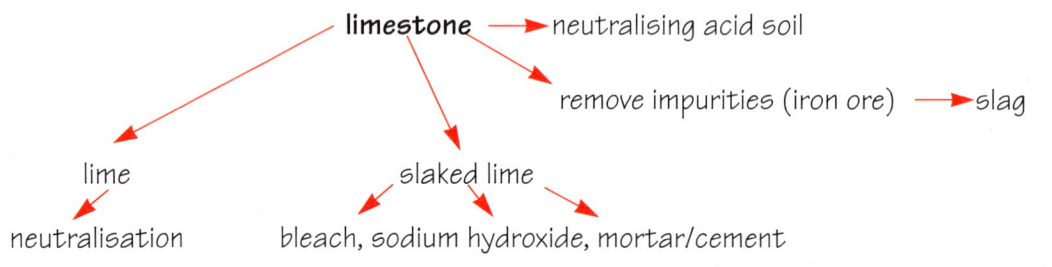

Glass is
Limestone
Along with
Sand and
Soda.

limestone → neutralising acid soil
           → remove impurities (iron ore) → slag
           ↓   ↓
         lime   slaked lime
           ↓   ↙   ↓   ↘
    neutralisation   bleach, sodium hydroxide, mortar/cement

Reactions involving enzymes

- Enzymes are **catalysts** made and used by **living cells**.
- Enable living cells to do a lot of chemical reactions – make new substances.
- **Yeast cells turn sugar into carbon dioxide and alcohol** – **fermentation**
  – in brewing – sugar in barley or grapes turned to alcohol in beer or wine
  – in baking bread – yeast → **carbon dioxide** bubbles in dough – makes bread 'rise'.
- Special bacteria turn sugar (lactose) in milk into lactic acid – sour taste in yoghurt.
- **Enzymes are large molecules of protein** – many amino acids linked together – these molecules are **damaged by higher temperatures** – above about 45 °C.
- Reactions involving **enzymes work best in warm conditions** – faster reactions – but not too hot to damage the enzymes – optimum temperature about 37 °C.
- Brewing – mixture of hops and yeast kept warm.
- Bread making – dough kept warm to rise – then heated strongly – baked – kills yeast.

PATTERNS OF BEHAVIOUR AND USING RAW MATERIALS

Useful products from oil

- **Crude oil** (**petroleum**) and **natural gas** – formed in Earth's crust.
- Small animals in ancient seas – died – sunk to sea bed – covered by sediment – changed by heat and pressure – no air present – became oil and natural gas – sediment became sedimentary rock.
- Porous (able to hold liquid) rocks can contain oil and gas on top of denser water.
- Some non-porous rock on top can trap oil and gas – for us to find.

- **Coal** formed on land – from similar process involving plant material.
- Oil, natural gas, coal are called **fossil fuels** – important raw materials.

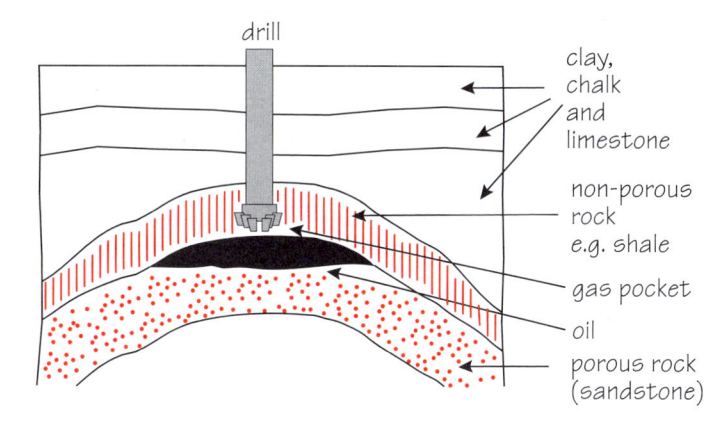

(Diagram labels: drill; clay, chalk and limestone; non-porous rock e.g. shale; gas pocket; oil; porous rock (sandstone))

- Crude oil is a **mixture** of different compounds – all are **hydrocarbons** – molecules containing carbon and hydrogen only.
- More useful if separated by **fractional distillation** into groups of compounds with a certain range of boiling points – groups of compounds called **fractions**.

Fractional distillation involves repeated evaporation and condensing.

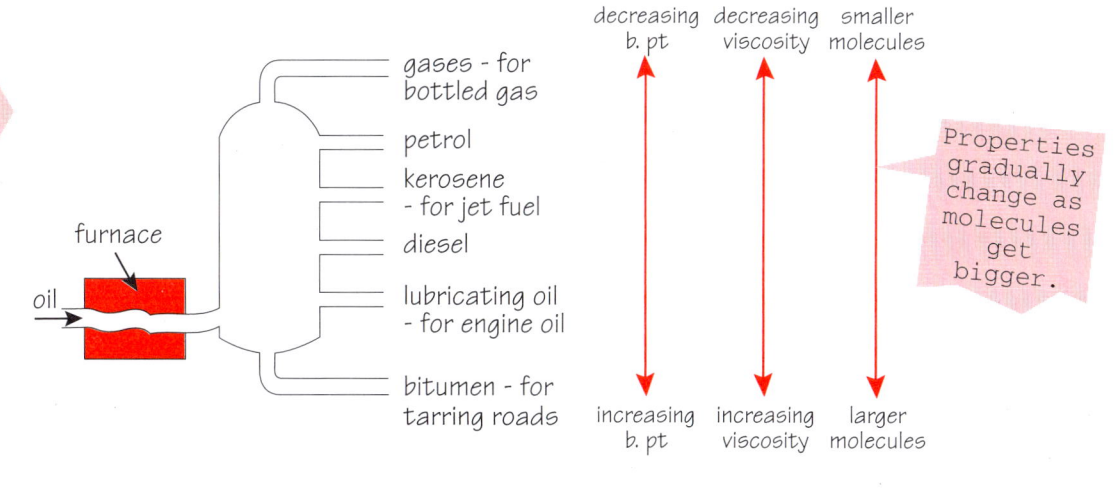

(Diagram: furnace, oil → fractionating column with outputs:
- *gases - for bottled gas*
- *petrol*
- *kerosene - for jet fuel*
- *diesel*
- *lubricating oil - for engine oil*
- *bitumen - for tarring roads*

Top: decreasing b. pt, decreasing viscosity, smaller molecules. Bottom: increasing b. pt, increasing viscosity, larger molecules.)

Properties gradually change as molecules get bigger.

- **Hydrocarbons** burn in good supply of air → **carbon dioxide** and **water**,
  e.g. methane + oxygen → carbon dioxide + water
  $$CH_{4(g)} + 2O_{2(g)} \rightarrow CO_{2(g)} + 2H_2O_{(g)}$$
- They are good fuels, e.g. propane in bottled gas, methane in natural gas.
- Burn in limited air supply giving **carbon monoxide** (poisonous) or even carbon (soot).
- Big hydrocarbon molecules need much more oxygen so are less good as fuels.
- Big molecules can be **cracked** (broken up) into smaller ones.
- Smaller molecules are more useful as fuels – burn easier and more cleanly.

63

MATERIALS AND THEIR PROPERTIES

Types of hydrocarbons – depends on how carbon atoms join – form spine of molecule.
Alkanes – all carbon atoms joined by **single covalent bonds**

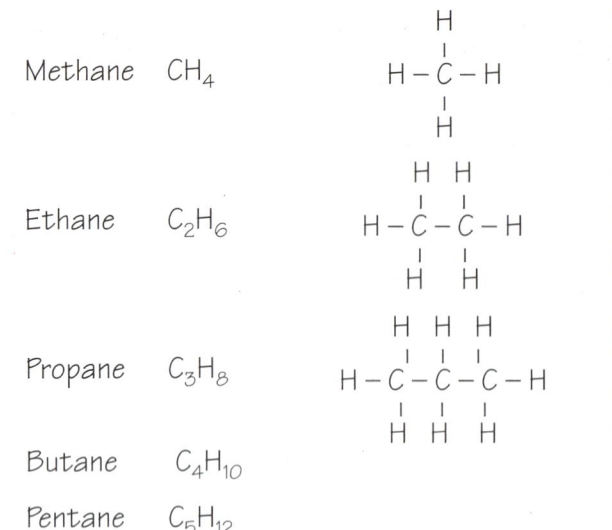

This is an example of an homologous series – they all have similar chemical properties – they all have a similar structure – names have same ending.

Methane CH_4

```
    H
    |
H - C - H
    |
    H
```

Ethane C_2H_6

```
  H   H
  |   |
H-C - C-H
  |   |
  H   H
```

Propane C_3H_8

```
  H   H   H
  |   |   |
H-C - C - C-H
  |   |   |
  H   H   H
```

Butane C_4H_{10}

Pentane C_5H_{12}

| goes up by CH_2 each time | properties e.g. density melting point gradually increase | become less volatile thicker harder to ignite |

Chemical properties of the alkanes:
- they burn to form carbon dioxide and water
- the bigger molecules can be **cracked** (broken down) by heat and a catalyst into smaller molecules (one of these is ethene – used in large amounts – see below)
- not very reactive – this is because they are **saturated** – contain all single bonds, e.g. react only **slowly** with bromine which gradually replaces the hydrogen in the molecule – so bromine water would not decolourise when mixed with an alkane:

$$CH_4 + Br_2 \rightarrow CH_3Br + HBr \quad \text{(reaction is a test for saturation)}$$

Alkenes – chain of carbon atoms contains **one double covalent bond**

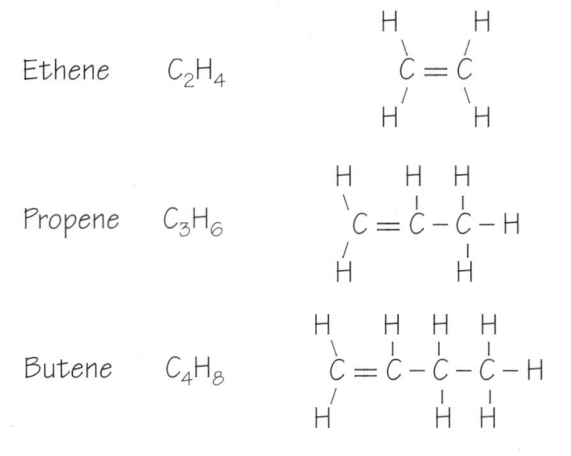

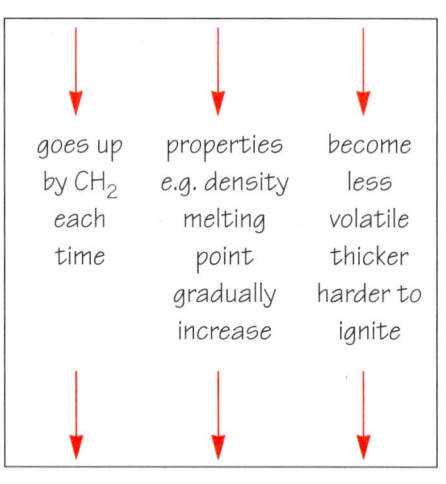

Another example of an homologous series.

Ethene C_2H_4

```
  H     H
   \   /
    C=C
   /   \
  H     H
```

Propene C_3H_6

```
  H   H   H
   \  |   |
    C=C - C-H
   /  |   |
  H   H   H
```

Butene C_4H_8

```
  H   H   H   H
   \  |   |   |
    C=C - C - C-H
   /  |   |   |
  H   H   H   H
```

| goes up by CH_2 each time | properties e.g. density melting point gradually increase | become less volatile thicker harder to ignite |

Chemical properties of the alkenes:
- they burn to form carbon dioxide and water
- very reactive – the double bond readily becomes a single bond and extra atoms can add onto the molecule,
  e.g. with bromine get a **rapid** reaction as the bromine adds to the molecule – so bromine water would rapidly decolourise

$$C_2H_4 + Br_2 \rightarrow C_2H_4Br_2 \quad \text{(reaction is a test for unsaturation)}$$

Ethene adds on to many substances – very useful in making compounds.

```
  H  H
  |  |
Cl-C- C-Cl         Cl_2                                Br_2            Br-C - C-Br
  |  |         ←                 H    H                      →           |  |
  H  H                            \  /                                   H  H
              H_2                  C=C              H_2O
            H  H                  /  \                           H   H
            |  |                 H    H                          |   |
          H-C- C-H              Ethene                         H-C - C-OH
            |  |                                                 |   |
            H  H                                                 H   H
```

Rate graphs

Comparing reaction conditions on a graph

Graph flattens when reaction complete.

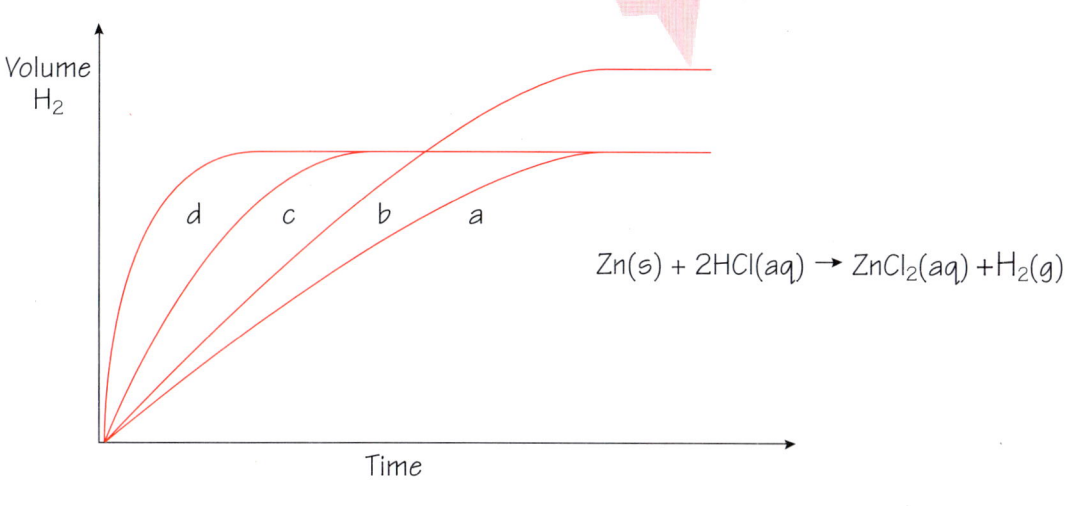

Zn(s) + 2HCl(aq) → ZnCl$_2$(aq) + H$_2$(g)

(Axes: Volume H$_2$ vs Time; curves labelled d, c, b, a from steepest to shallowest)

- c – reference graph (2 g Zn pieces with excess acid).
- d – same amounts – powdered zinc/catalyst added (CuSO$_4$) or higher temperature.
- a – large piece of zinc (2 g)/weaker acid.
- b – more zinc used with excess acid.

Energy changes in chemical reactions

- **Exothermic** reactions – energy **given out** – temperature **rise** – ΔH = **negative**.
- **Endothermic** reactions – energy **taken in** – temperature **drop** – ΔH = **positive**.

Energy diagram:

You must be able to draw energy diagrams.

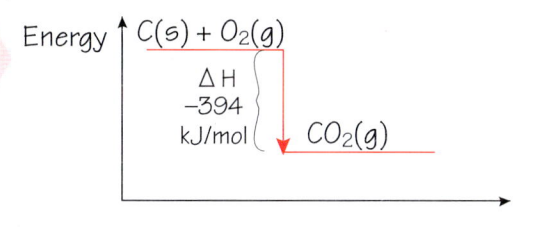

Exothermic reaction

Energy: C(s) + O$_2$(g) → CO$_2$(g), ΔH = −394 kJ/mol

e.g. **all** burning fuels

Endothermic reaction

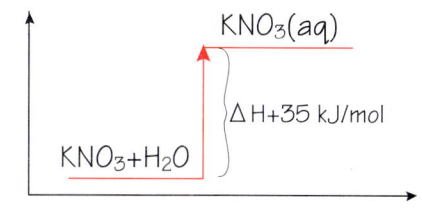

KNO$_3$(aq) ← KNO$_3$ + H$_2$O, ΔH = +35 kJ/mol

Potassium nitrate (aq)

Note: Most reactions are exothermic.

During a chemical reaction

- Energy must be supplied to break bonds.
- Energy is released when bonds form.

MATERIALS AND THEIR PROPERTIES

Exothermic

Energy
reactants
products
Reaction pathway

Endothermic

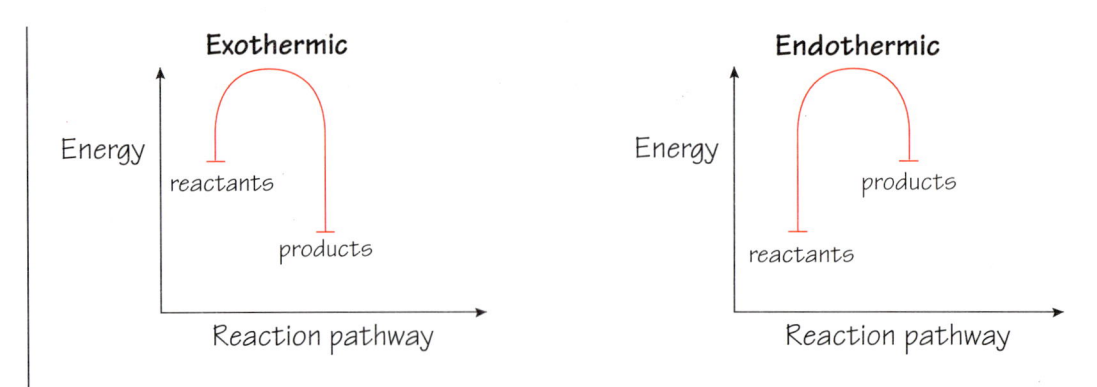

Energy
products
reactants
Reaction pathway

Calculating energy changes

Can use formulae and equations to calculate how much energy is used and how much is formed in a chemical reaction.
For this we use **bond energies**.

> You may not need to break every bond in reactions.

Example of a calculation:
$CH_4 + 2O_2 \rightarrow CO_2 + 2H_2O$

- Calculate the energy change – is reaction endo/exothermic?
  Bond energy: C–H = 413, O=O = 498, C=O = 803, O–H = 463 kJ/mol.
- Calculate total energy to break the bonds (**+**):
  4 C–H bonds = 4 × 413 = 1652
  2 O=O bonds = 2 × 498 = 996
  Total = 2648 kJ.
- Calculate the total energy when bonds are formed:
  2 C=O bonds = 2 × 803 = 1606
  4 O–H bonds = 4 × 463 = 1852
  Total 3458 kJ.

> Relate 810 kJ to exothermic energy diagram.

> Don't forget the **sign** (+ or −) and **units**.

- **Net change** = + 2648 − 3458 = − 810 kJ.
- Reaction is **exothermic** – **heat absorbed** when bonds of CH_4 and O_2 broken **less than heat given out** when bonds of CO_2 and H_2O formed.

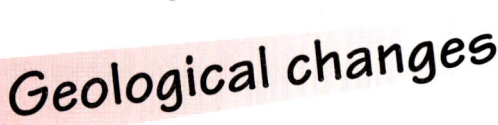

Geological changes

3 types of rock – igneous, sedimentary and metamorphic.

- **Igneous rocks** – **cooling** down of molten rock (**magma**) → random, interlocking **crystals** of different minerals.
  – Slow cooling (within Earth's crust) – large crystals, easily seen – **intrusive** rock, e.g. **granite**.
  – Rapid cooling (erupted from volcanoes) – small crystals, seen under microscope – **extrusive** rock, e.g. **basalt**.

- **Sedimentary** rocks – **deposition** of sediments in **layers** followed by **compression** – pressure of layers above – squeezes out water – **cementation** of sediment particles → rock, e.g. **chalk, limestone, sandstone, mudstone**.
- May contain **fossils** – remains of plants, animals trapped between layers (often shelly) – used to identify and date rocks.

- **Metamorphic** rocks – action of **heat** and **pressure** on existing rocks,
  e.g. limestone to **marble**, mudstone to **slate** and **schist** (banded rock with interlocking crystals).

MATERIALS AND THEIR PROPERTIES

- Movement of tectonic plates → mountain building and burial of rocks deep underground – become heated and compressed → metamorphic rock.

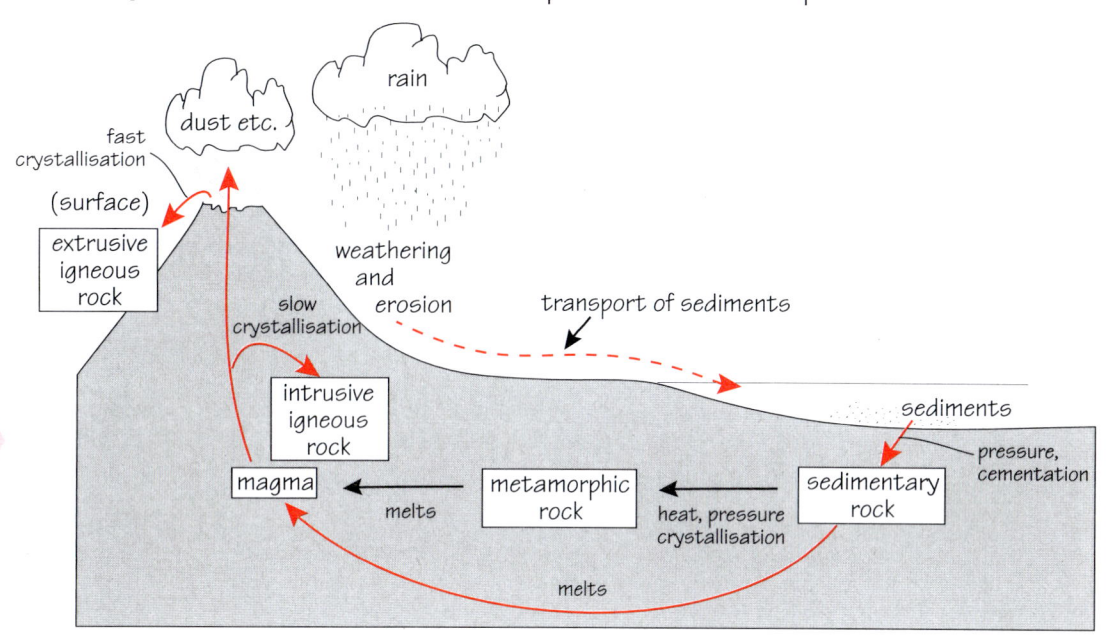

Diagram of rock cycle usually given – learn labels.

You must be able to explain how it happens.

- **Weathering** and **erosion** also responsible for **recycling** of surface rock.
- Weathering – **breakdown** of rock by water, wind, animals, plant roots, chemicals.
- Erosion – **carrying away** of rock by water, wind, gravity.

Plate tectonics

Structure of the Earth – evidence from earthquake waves:

- **S and P shock waves allow structure of Earth to be worked out**
  – **fast P waves** travel through **liquids and solids**
  – **slow S waves** travel only in **solids**.

Size of earthquake measured on the Richter scale.

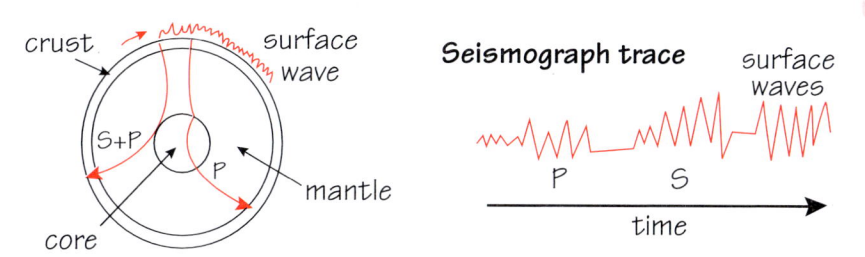

The Earth has:
- a thin **crust** (about 20 km thick)
- a **mantle** – very viscous liquid
- a dense **core** (just over half Earth's radius) made of **nickel** and **iron** – origin of Earth's magnetic field – outer core liquid, inner core solid
- **crust is less dense** than overall density of Earth – shows interior of Earth made of different and denser material.

Changes to the atmosphere

- **Volcanic activity** – first billion years of Earth's existence – released gases → original atmosphere.
- Contained carbon dioxide, methane, ammonia, water vapour → condensed → oceans (little/no oxygen present).

67

MATERIALS AND THEIR PROPERTIES

- **Plants evolved** – photosynthesis developed – changed carbon dioxide into oxygen → used in respiration – carbon locked in plants, formed fossil fuels.
- Methane and ammonia reacted with oxygen → nitrogen.
- **Living organisms** and **denitrifying** bacteria made more nitrogen.
- Oxygen led to development of **ozone layer** – filters harmful UV rays from sunlight – new organisms could evolve.
- Carbon dioxide absorbed by sea water → sediments of carbonate rocks and soluble hydrogencarbonates (mainly calcium and magnesium).
- Composition of atmosphere maintained by **carbon cycle** – animals, plants and microorganisms.

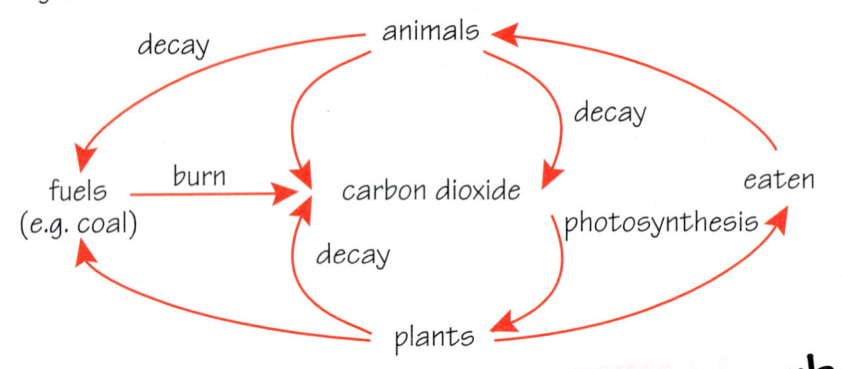

Crude oil (petroleum) and hydrocarbons

- Crude oil (petroleum) – formed in several steps over **millions of years**: sea creatures die → sink to sea bed → covered by rock → heat and pressure causes them to decay → oil and gas.
- Crude oil can be separated into **fractions** according to their **boiling points** by **fractional distillation**.

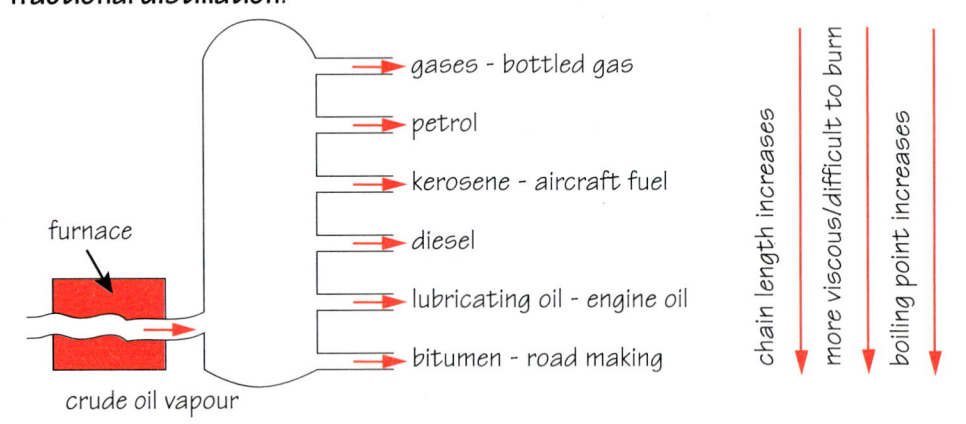

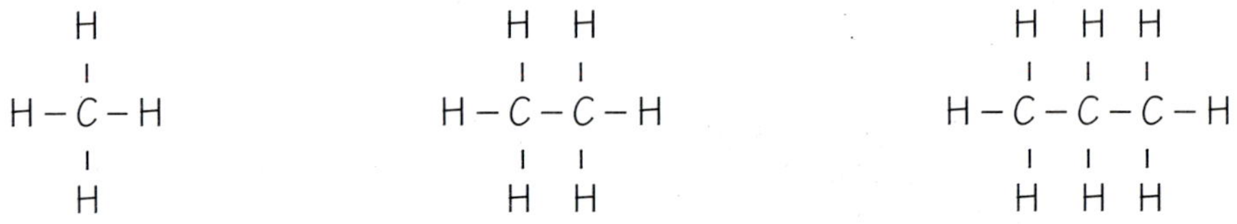

Fractions (top to bottom):
- gases - bottled gas
- petrol
- kerosene - aircraft fuel
- diesel
- lubricating oil - engine oil
- bitumen - road making

chain length increases, more viscous/difficult to burn, boiling point increases (going down)

- Crude oil contains **hydrocarbons**.
- Hydrocarbons contain **only hydrogen** and **carbon**. *(Key word **only**.)*
- They **burn** in a **good** supply of air (oxygen) to form **carbon dioxide** and **water**.
- In a **limited** supply of air → **carbon monoxide** formed (**very poisonous**).

Saturated hydrocarbons → alkanes

- Molecules in which carbon atoms are linked by single **C–C covalent bonds**, e.g. methane (g), ethane (g), propane (g)

methane:
```
    H
    |
H – C – H
    |
    H
```

ethane:
```
  H   H
  |   |
H-C – C-H
  |   |
  H   H
```

propane:
```
  H   H   H
  |   |   |
H-C – C – C-H
  |   |   |
  H   H   H
```

Unsaturated hydrocarbons → alkenes

- Molecules in which carbon atoms are linked by **double C=C bonds**,

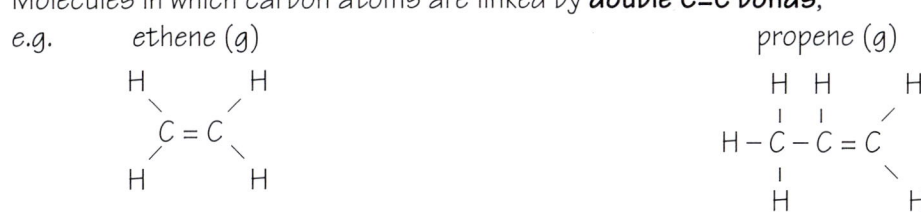

  e.g. ethene (g)   propene (g)

  [structure of ethene: H₂C=CH₂]   [structure of propene: CH₃–CH=CH₂]

- React by breaking double bond and other atoms added on – **addition reactions** – bonds become single,

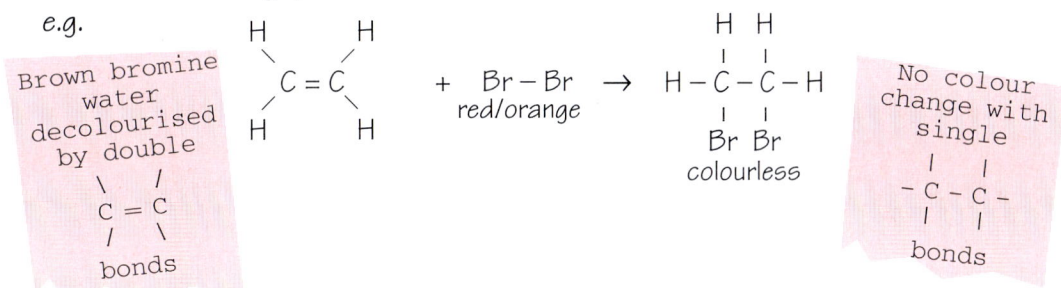

  e.g.

  > Brown bromine water decolourised by double \\C=C/ /C=C\\ bonds

  H₂C=CH₂ + Br–Br (red/orange) → H–CHBr–CHBr–H (Br Br colourless)

  > No colour change with single –C–C– bonds

  Br₂ – used to test for C=C bonds.

Cracking

Process in which large hydrocarbon molecules are **broken down** into **smaller, more useful molecules**. High temperature, high pressure and catalyst needed.

E.g.

    Word equation   decane → octane   + ethene
                                    for petrol   (to make polyethene)

    Chemical equation $C_{10}H_{22}$ → C_8H_{18} + C_2H_4

Macromolecules

- Very large molecules which have very useful properties.

Two types:

- **addition polymers** – large number of small molecules (monomers) **join together** → polymer → process called polymerisation

  n CH₂=CH₂ → –(CH₂–CH₂)–ₙ poly(ethene)

  monomer   polymer ($n > 50$)

- **condensation polymers** – monomers join together to form a large chain and a small molecule, e.g. water, **is given out**

  n (H₂N–☐–NH₂   +   HOOC–☐–COOH) → (–NH–☐–NH–CO–☐–CO–)ₙ

  monomer 1   monomer 2   polymer + nH_2O

- **Synthetic** polymers, e.g. nylon, polyester.
- **Natural** polymers, e.g. starch (**monomer – glucose**), proteins (**monomers – amino acids**).

Materials and their properties

Questions

1 In an experiment it was found that 1.12 g of iron reacted with 2.13 g of chlorine. Calculate the formula of the compound formed (relative atomic mass: Fe = 56, Cl = 35.5).

_____
_____
_____
_____

2 A molten electrolyte contains sodium ions, Na^+ and chloride ions, Cl^-.
(**a**) Explain why the electrolyte conducts electricity.

_____
_____

(**b**) Chloride ions, Cl^-, react at the anode.
The equation for the reaction is: _____

This is an example of oxidation. Explain why.

_____

3 A hydrocarbon, propane (C_3H_8), was burned in a plentiful supply of air (oxygen).
(**a**) Write a word and a balanced chemical equation for the reaction.
word equation _____
chemical equation _____

(**b**) A hydrocarbon is a substance which contains _____ and _____ only.

(**c**) Crude oil can be _____ into _____ by the process of
_____

4 The amount of carbon dioxide and oxygen in the atmosphere stays roughly constant.
Green plants take in _____ and change it into food and _____
This process is called _____. When fossil fuels are burned _____ is used up.

5 Ammonia is formed from hydrogen and nitrogen.

$$N_2(g) + 3H_2(g) \rightleftharpoons 2NH_3(g) \quad \Delta H = -92 \text{ kJ/mol}$$

Explain how the equilibrium could be shifted to the left (increasing reactants).

_____
_____
_____

Answers

Materials and their properties
Classifying materials

1 (a) 7, 3, (2, 1)
   7, 3, 4, 2 (2)
   6, 6 (2, 4)
   7, 6 (2, 4)
   20, 10 (2, 8)
   16, 16, (2, 8, 8)

   (b) Li^+, Ne and S^{2-}

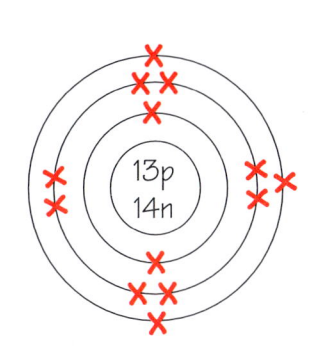

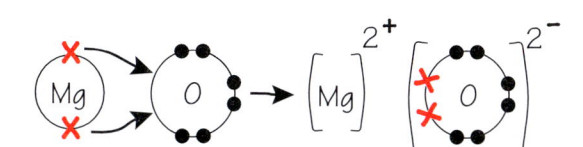

2 [diagram: atom with 13p 14n nucleus and electron shells 2,8,3]

3 [diagram: Mg atom transferring 2 electrons to O atom, forming $[Mg]^{2+}$ and $[O]^{2-}$]

4 Protons, electrons

5 (a) A
   (b) C
   (c) B

Patterns of behaviour

1 (a) A/B/C/D   (b) E   (c) D   (d) $2Ca + O_2 \rightarrow 2CaO$ 2 (a) Group 1, alkali metals, under oil, reacts, water   (b) floats, moves on surface, fumes, cloudy solution
3 Haber process, ammonia   4 Noble gases, react, 8 (0)   5 Group 7, halogens $Cl_2 + 2Br^- \rightarrow 2Cl^- + Br_2$, displacement reaction   6 Hard, high density, catalysts
7 (a) bromine   (b) sodium chloride   (c) silver bromide

Materials and their properties

1 mol Fe = 1.12/56 = 0.02   mol Cl = 2.13/35.5 = 0.06   Ratio Fe : Cl = 1 : 3, formula $FeCl_3$ 2 (a) Ions are free to move about.   (b) $2Cl^- \rightarrow Cl_2 + 2e^-$ or $2Cl^- - 2e^- \rightarrow Cl_2$ or $Cl^- \rightarrow Cl + e$ electrons are being lost.   3 (a) propane + oxygen → carbon dioxide + water $C_3H_8 + 5O_2 \rightarrow 3CO_2 + 4H_2O$ (b) Hydrogen, carbon
(c) Separated, fractions, fractional distillation   4 Carbon dioxide, oxygen, photosynthesis, oxygen   5 Any of following: increasing the temperature, decreasing the pressure, removing the reactants, adding more ammonia

Physical processes

Electricity and magnetism

Electrostatics

- **Static electricity** – electric charges **stationary**.
- **Charges** – **positive** (+) or **negative** (–).
- **Insulators** – substances in which **electricity cannot flow**, e.g. plastics.
- **Conductors** – substances in which **electricity can flow**, e.g. metals.
- **Electron transfer** – two insulators rubbed together.
- **Insulator + electrons → negative charge** (–).
- **Insulator – electrons → positive charge** (+).

Charged objects

- **Like charges repel** + and + or – and –.
- **Unlike charges attract** + and –.
- **Charged objects attract uncharged** objects.

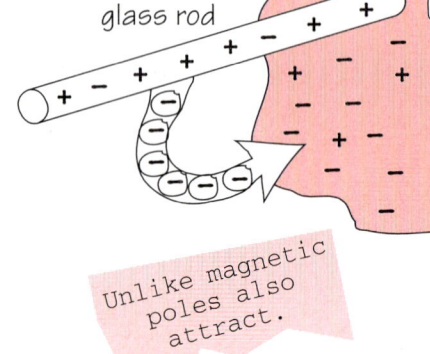

Unlike magnetic poles also attract.

Applications

You need to be able to describe dangers and uses.

Electrostatic filters – used to clean smoky chimneys.
Aircraft fuel lines – earthed to avoid sparks/fire.

Electrolysis

- **Ionic compounds**, e.g. sodium chloride NaCl **conduct electricity** when molten or dissolved in water.
- **Negative (–) ions flow to anode** (positive electrode).
- **Positive (+) ions flow to cathode** (negative electrode).
- **Substances deposited/released at electrodes.**
- Amount of substance deposited/released greater when
  - the size of the current greater
  - the time for which the current flows greater.

Current electricity

Resistance

- **Current electricity** – (negative) electric charges **move**.
- **Resistance** – anything that **hinders movement**.
- **Resistance of conductor greater** – conductor **longer or thinner**
  – conductor **hotter**.
- **Resistance different** – different materials, e.g. copper and lead.
- Resistance = $\dfrac{\text{voltage}}{\text{current}}$
- **Units** – ohms (Ω).
- **Ohm's law** – voltage proportional to current.

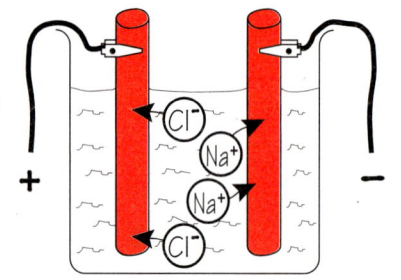

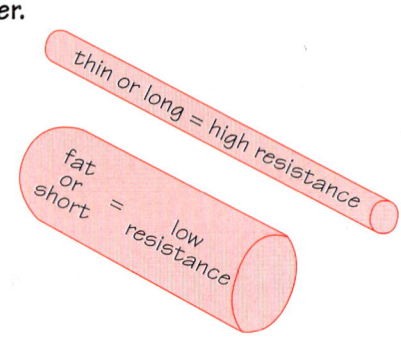

thin or long = high resistance
fat or short = low resistance

72

ELECTRICITY AND MAGNETISM

Graphs should have a label and unit on each axis.

Current – voltage graphs for different components

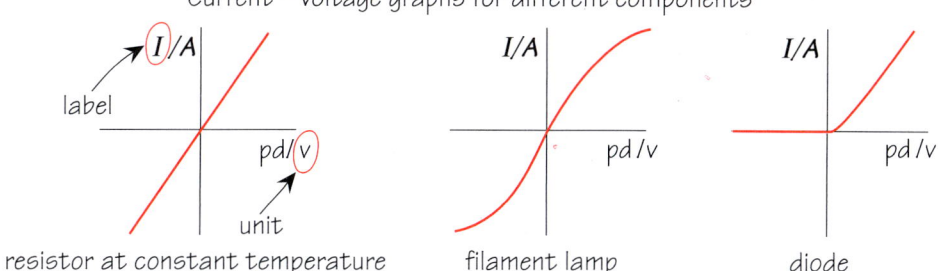

- resistor at constant temperature
- filament lamp
- diode

(label: I/A, unit: pd/V)

- **Ohmic conductor** – **resistance constant** (graph a) e.g. metal wire.
- **Non-ohmic conductor** – **resistance varies** (graph b) e.g. lamp filament
  – resistance thermistor decreases as temperature rises
  – resistance LDR decreases as light level rises.

- **Series resistors** $R = R_1 + R_2$
  – current same
  – potential difference (pd) divided up.

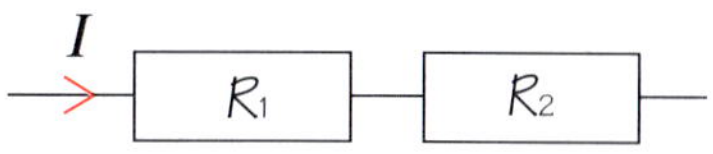

- **Parallel resistors** $\dfrac{1}{R} = \dfrac{1}{R_1} + \dfrac{1}{R_2}$
  – current divided $I = I_1 + I_2$
  – pd same.

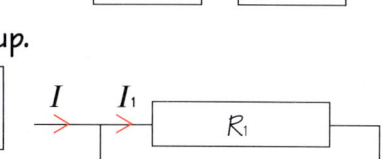

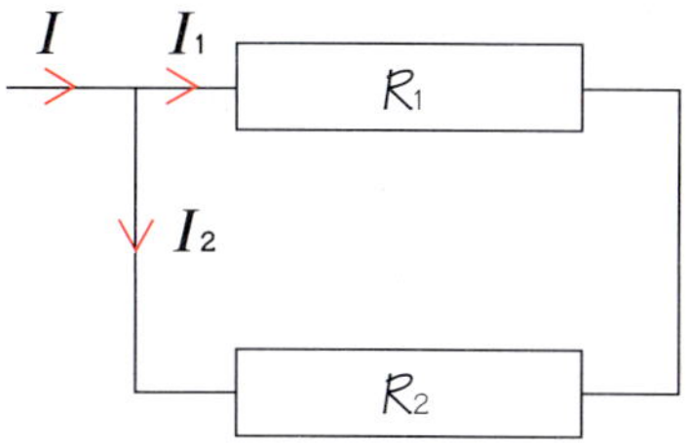

Note that 'I' is the symbol for current. 'A' stands for Amperes (Amps).

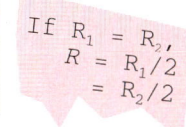

If $R_1 = R_2$, $R = R_1/2 = R_2/2$

Using electricity

Energy in circuits

- Electric current – flow of charge.
- Energy – **given to each electron** by battery/power supply.
- More energy – (pd) higher.
- 1 V – 1 J per coulomb of charge (C).
- 1 A – current when 1 C flows/second.
- Energy transfer –
  $\boxed{\text{Power} = \text{pd} \times \text{current}}$ = energy transfer/second.
- Units of power – 1 W = 1 J/s.

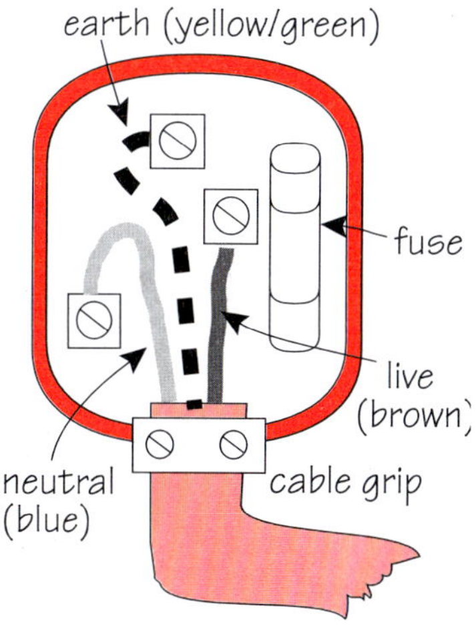

earth (yellow/green), fuse, live (brown), cable grip, neutral (blue)

Safety

There is usually a question on plugs and/or fuses.

- **Fuse** – low melting-point wire.
- **Plug** – 3-pin plug needs **correct fuse**.
- **Fuse size** – use I = P/V where p is the power rating in Watts.
- High current e.g. 12 A – **large fuse**, 13 A.
- Low current e.g. 1 A – **small fuse**, 2 A.
- Circuit breaker – instead of fuse.

- Metal case – **appliance must be earthed.**
- Plastic case – **extra protection.**
  – said to be **'double insulated'**.

Application of heating effect in a resistor

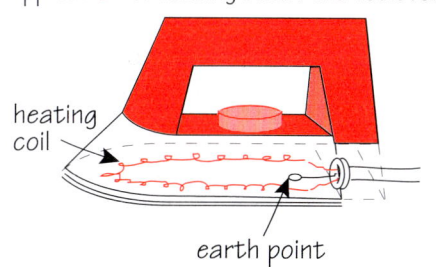

heating coil, earth point

If live wire loose large current → earth.

Cost

- Unit – kilowatt hour (kWh).
- Kilowatt – 1000 watts.
- Total cost – $\boxed{\text{number of units} \times \text{cost per unit}}$
- Example – 3 kW for 3 hours = 9 units
  9 units @ 6p = 54p.

73

PHYSICAL PROCESSES

Electromagnetism

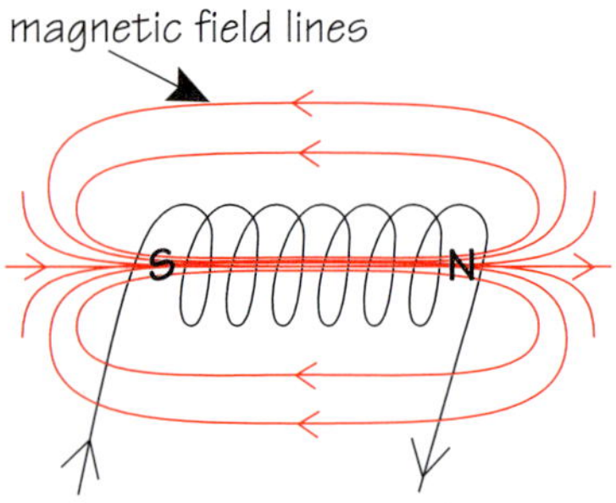

Magnets

- Like poles repel, unlike attract.

Electromagnets

Examiners often set questions on applications to show an understanding of the principles.

- **Electromagnet** – coil of wire with electric current.
- **Strength** of an electromagnet **increased by**
  - placing an **iron core** in it
  - **increasing the number of turns of wire**
  - **increasing size of current** through it.

Applications:
- **electric bell** – hammer attracted by electromagnet when current flows
- **relay** – switch closed when electromagnet activated.

Note that it behaves like a bar magnet.

magnetic field lines

Electromagnetic forces

- Force on wire in magnetic field.
- Direction of force –
  - Fleming's **Left Hand Rule**
  - **direction** of force **reverses** if **current reverses**.
- **Size of force increases with**
  - strength of **magnetic field**
  - size of **current**
  - increased **number of turns of wire**.

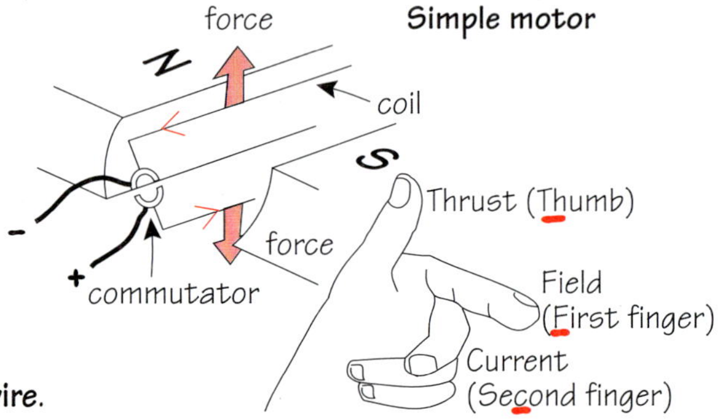

Applications:
- **motors** – force produces **rotary movement** e.g. electric drill, washing machine
- **loudspeakers** – **cone forced in and out** to produce sound waves
- **circuit breakers** – high current activates electromagnet.

Simple motor — Thrust (Thumb), Field (First finger), Current (Second finger)

Electromagnetic induction

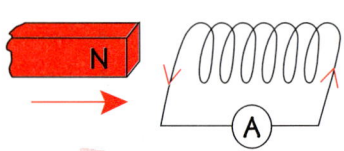

- Magnet → coil of wire – current induced.
- Coil of wire → magnet – current induced.
- No movement – no current.

Applications:
- **generator/dynamo** – produces electricity
- **transformers** (see below) – **change size** of a **voltage**.

Use the right hand rule to find the direction of the current in a generator.

Alternating current

- **Direct current** (dc) – electrons move in one direction.
- Batteries produce dc.
- **Alternating current** (ac) – electrons change direction.
- Power stations produce ac.

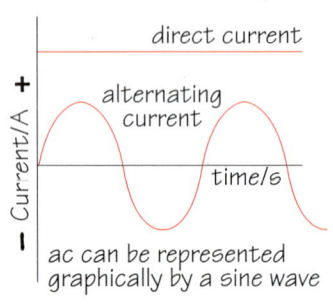

ac can be represented graphically by a sine wave

Transformers

- **High current** – a lot of **heat**.
- **High voltage** – avoid heat loss.
- **Power stations** – produce electricity at **high voltage**.
- **Transformers** – **step down** (or **up**) **voltages**
  - work on ac not dc.
- **Electricity at home** – **240 V ac** (in UK).

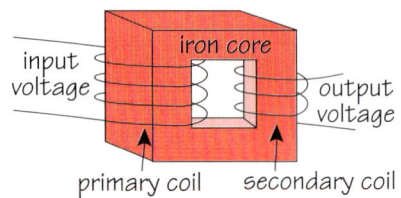

secondary pd = primary pd x no. secondary turns/no. primary turns

74

Electricity and magnetism
Questions

1. In terms of charge transfer, describe what happens when you rub a glass rod with a silk cloth. _____

2. In this circuit, the two lamps are identical.
   (a) What is the pd across each lamp? _____ V
   (b) If the current flow in the main part of the circuit is 3.0 A, calculate the resistance of each lamp filament.
   _____

3. An electric kettle is rated at 1.5 kW.
   (a) Assuming that the domestic voltage supply is 250 V, what is the correct-sized fuse for the plug? (Choose from the following sizes: 1 A, 2 A, 3 A, 5 A, 10 A, 13 A.) _____

   (b) A unit of electricity costs 6p. How much does it cost to operate the kettle each day for a week, 20 minutes a day? _____

4. (a) What is meant by a step-up transformer? _____

   (b) The primary coil of a transformer has 100 turns. A pd of 2.0 V is applied across it. If an output voltage of 7.0 V is needed, how many turns of wire should the secondary coil have? _____

PHYSICAL PROCESSES

Forces and motion
Representing motion

Distance – time graphs

- Speed = distance/time
- Units – m/s (ms^{-1}).
- Graph a – **stationary** body.
- Graphs b and c – **steady** speed.
- Gradient → speed.
- b faster than c.

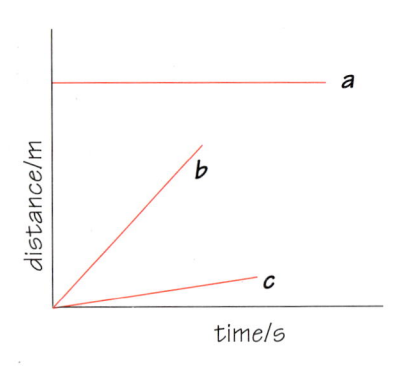

Velocity – time graphs

- Acceleration = change in velocity/time taken

Examiners usually set questions on drawing or interpreting graphs.

- Units – m/s² (ms^{-2}).
- Graph a – **constant velocity**.
- Graphs b and c – **constant acceleration**.
- Gradient → acceleration.
- b greater acceleration than c.

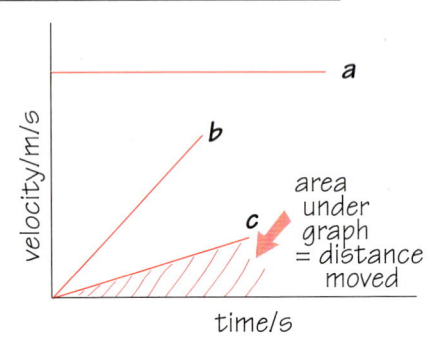

area under graph = distance moved

Force – extension graphs

- Linear part – $F \propto e$ (Hooke's Law).
- OA – **elastic** region
- AB – **plastic** region
- B – **yield point**; wire stretches with little load
- C – **breaking point**.

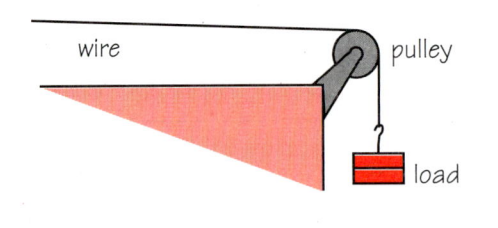

Balanced forces

- Weight, W – **downwards** on table.
- Force, R – **upwards** on book.
- R = W – forces balance
  — book **stationary**.

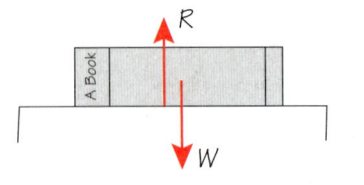

Other (frictional) forces also act on the car.

- Thrust, T – car pushed through air.
- Force, R – air drag on car.
- R = T – forces balance
  — car **constant speed**.

- W greater than R → book falls!
- T greater than R → car accelerates!
- Forces unbalanced.
- Unbalanced forces – change in motion.
- Force = mass × acceleration
- Units – Newtons (N).
- 1 N – 1 kg m/s².

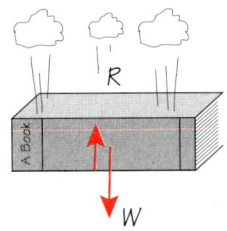

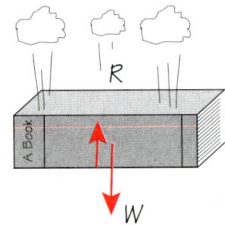

76

FORCES AND MOTION

Friction

You need to be able to state or describe both advantages and disadvantages.

- Friction acts
  - between two **surfaces that move**
  - when **body moves through gas or liquid**.
- Friction – **opposes motion**
  - causes **heating/wear**, e.g. car engine
  - **needed** for moving and stopping.

Road safety

- Stopping distance depends on
  - driver **reaction time**
  - **braking distance**.
- Braking distance depends on
  - **speed**
  - **tyres**
  - **brakes**
  - **road surface**.

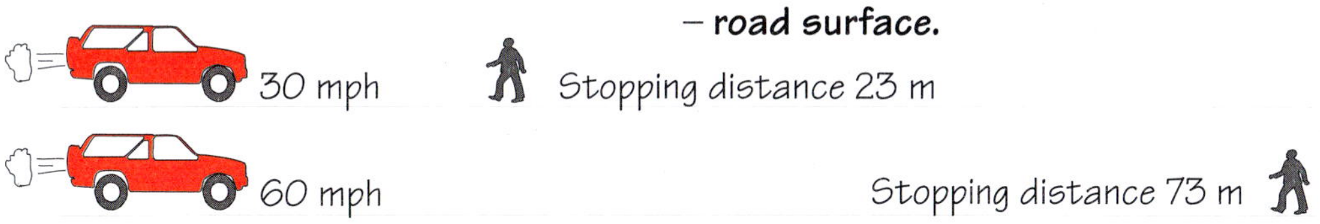

30 mph — Stopping distance 23 m

60 mph — Stopping distance 73 m

Free fall

- Weight → **acceleration**.
- Air drag, R – **increases** with speed.
- R = W → terminal velocity.
- Terminal velocity – **constant**
  - **zero acceleration**
  - about **170 mph** in air.

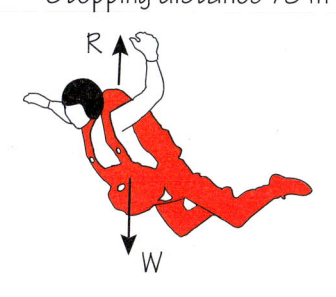

Turning forces

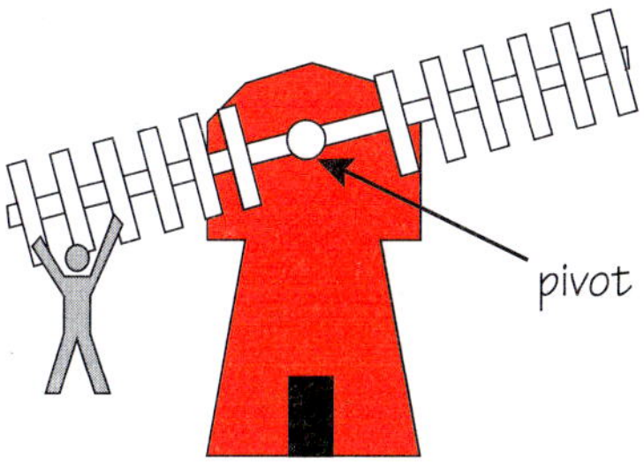

- Weight – **windmill turns**.
- Turning effect greater if
  - **weight** (or force) **greater**
  - **distance** to pivot is **greater**.
- Turning effect = force × perpendicular distance to pivot
- **Moment** – another name for **turning effect**.

- **Centre of mass** – where body **balances**
- LH force/s – turn beam ↺
- RH force/s – turn beam ↻
- balance – ↺ moments = ↻ moments

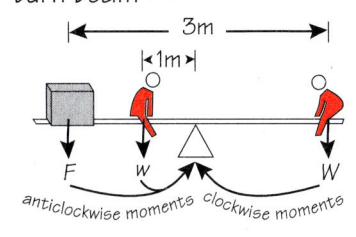

Words clockwise and anticlockwise don't need to appear if symbols ↻ and ↺ do.

$F \times 1.5 + w \times 1 = W \times 1.5$

anticlockwise moments / clockwise moments

Stability increases if centre of mass is nearer ground, e.g. sports car.

- **Stable** – weight line inside base.
- **Unstable** – **falls** if pushed
  - weight line outside base.
- **Neutral** – centre of mass stays same height.

c = centre of mass

stable — unstable — neutral equilibrium

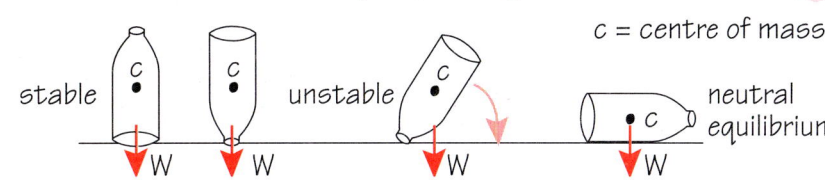

PHYSICAL PROCESSES

Momentum

Remember to quote correct units in a calculation.

- Momentum = mass x velocity
- Units – kg m/s.
- Collision/explosion – –ve force = +ve force → momentum change.
- Conservation – momentum before = momentum after
  – KE usually less after collision → heat/sound.

Planetary orbits are not perfectly circular; they are elliptical.

Circular motion

Stability

- Circular path – direction changes → velocity changes → acceleration.
- Centripetal force – acts on body since $f = m \times a$
  – acts **towards centre**.
- Centripetal force greater if
  – **mass** of body **greater**
  – **speed** of body **greater**
  – **radius** of circle **smaller**.
- Examples – planetary motion/motion of **satellites**
  – car rounding a bend.

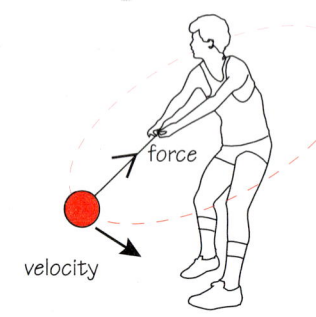

Pressure

Solids

- Pressure = force/area
- Units – N/m^2.
- $1 N/m^2$ = 1 pascal (Pa).
- Stiletto heel – small area.
- Small area → high pressure.
- Snow skis – large area.
- Large area → low pressure.

Example of high pressure

Example of low pressure

Liquids

- Pressure = $d \times h \times g$
- d – density   density = mass/volume
- h – depth.
- g – gravitational field strength (10 N/kg).
- Pressure – **equal** in all directions.

A dam is thicker at its base

Example:
- **hydraulic system** – e.g. car jack, car brakes
- **master piston A** – transmits pressure
- **brake piston B** – **pressed** by liquid – has **larger area**
- $P = F/A$ → force α area
- **force exerted** – **larger**
  – magnified by ratio of area B/area A.

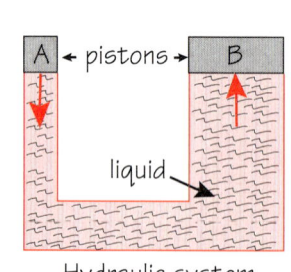

Hydraulic system

This is the important bit to remember in calculations.

Gases

You should be able to explain gas pressure in terms of particles colliding with container walls.

- **Volume** of gas – **decreases** when **pressure increases**.
- **Temperature** – constant.
- Mathematically – V α 1/P → Boyle's Law
  – $P_1V_1 = P_2V_2$.

- Example – **bicycle pump** – press on piston
  – volume of air decreases.

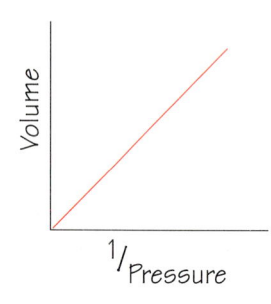

78

Forces and motion
Questions

1. A lorry starts from rest. A velocity – time graph of its motion is drawn for the first 30 seconds.
   (a) Describe its motion _____
   _____

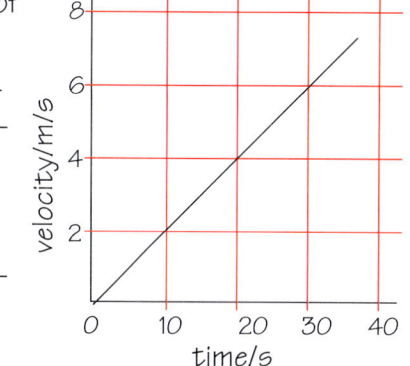

   (b) Calculate
      i) its acceleration _____
      _____

      ii) the distance moved _____
      _____

2. The mass of a sports car is 1200 kg. The engine provides a thrust of 6500 N. Over a measured course, the average air drag is found to be 850 N.
   (a) What acceleration is produced? _____
   _____

   (b) What does the total stopping distance depend upon? _____
   _____

3. A uniform beam of length 2.5 m is used to weigh sacks of flour. A weight of 120 N has to be placed at point X for it to balance. X is 0.5 m from the pivot.
   What is the weight of the flour? _____
   _____

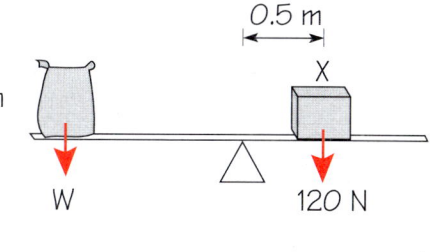

4. Bus A of mass 5000 kg is travelling east at 10 m/s. At the same time, bus B of mass 3000 kg is travelling in the same direction at 5 m/s. When they collide A and B move together as one. At what speed will they continue to move?
   _____
   _____
   _____

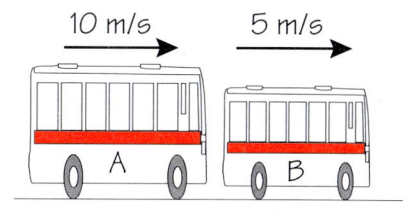

5. In a car brake system, the brake pedal pushes on a master piston of area 0.1 m^2 with a force of 150 N. If the brake piston is of area 0.4 m^2, what force is exerted on the wheels to stop them?
   _____
   _____

PHYSICAL PROCESSES

Waves

- **Waves transfer energy** not matter.

direction of travel — *crest* — λ — *amplitude* — *vibration* — *trough*

Transverse waves

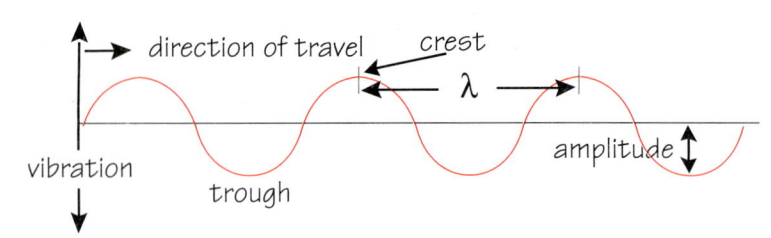

- Examples – **water, light, radio**.
- Vibration – **90° to direction of travel**.
- Wavelength (λ) – from **one crest to the next**.
- Frequency – **number of waves per second**; 1 Hz = 1 wave/sec.
- Electromagnetic waves e.g. **light can travel in a vacuum**.

Period is time for one cycle; frequency = $\frac{1}{\text{period}}$

Longitudinal waves

- Examples – **sound, slinky spring** as diagram below.
- Vibration – **same direction as travel**.
- Wavelength – from **one compression to the next**.
- **Sound travels in solids, liquids, gases but not a vacuum**.

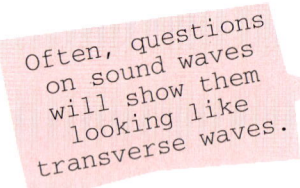

Often, questions on sound waves will show them looking like transverse waves.

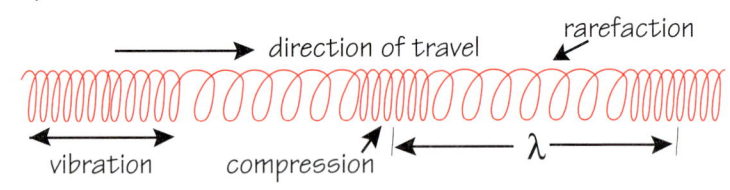

direction of travel — *rarefaction* — *vibration* — *compression* — λ

- **Wavespeed = wavelength × frequency** $v = \lambda \times f$

Properties of waves

Reflection

Remember arrows on diagram show direction of the light.

- Angle *i* = angle *r* for all waves.
- Mirror image – virtual
  – same size
  – upright
  – OM = MI.

A quick way to draw this accurately:-
1) draw object + 2 incident rays
2) since OM = MI, draw in image
3) draw dotted lines joining incident rays to image
4) extend dotted lines as rays on LH side of mirror.

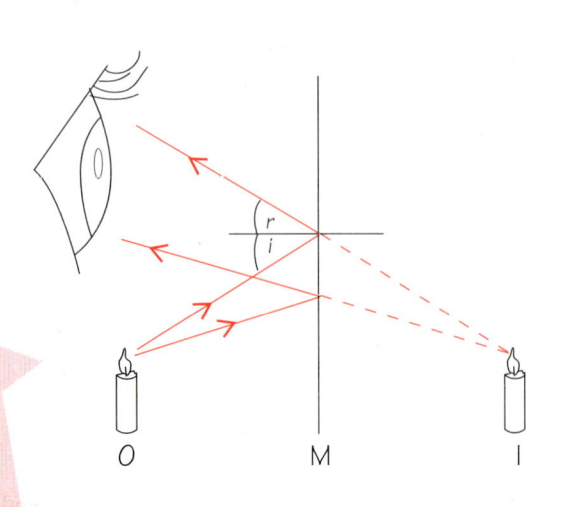

80

Waves

- **Waves transfer energy** not matter.

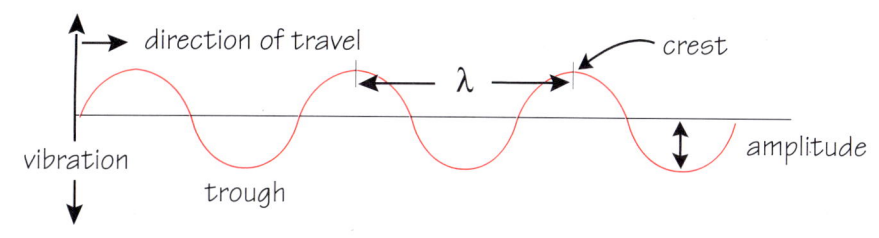

Transverse waves

- Examples – **water, light, radio**.
- Vibration – **90° to direction of travel**.
- Wavelength (λ) – from **one crest to the next**.
- Frequency – **number of waves per second**; 1 Hz = 1 wave/sec.
- Electromagnetic waves e.g. light **can travel in a vacuum**.

Longitudinal wave

- Examples – **sound, slinky spring** as diagram below.
- Vibration – **same direction as travel**.
- Wavelength – from **one compression to the next**.
- **Sound travels in solids, liquids, gases but not a vacuum.**

Often, questions on sound waves will show them looking like transverse waves.

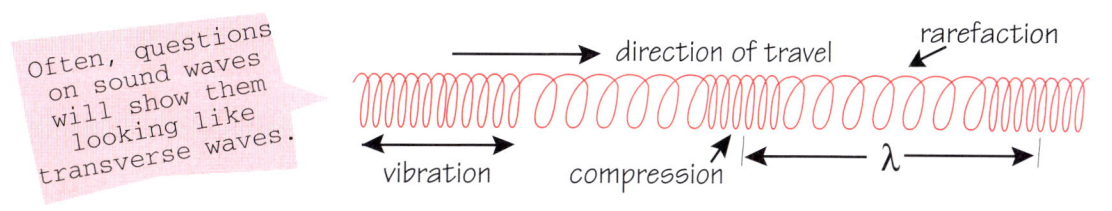

- **Wavespeed = wavelength x frequency** ; $v = \lambda \times f$

Properties of waves

Reflection

Remember arrows on diagram show direction of the light.

- Angle i = angle r for all waves.
- Mirror image – **virtual**
  – same size
  – upright
  – OM = MI.

A quick way to draw this accurately:
1) draw object + 2 incident rays
2) since OM = MI, draw in image
3) draw dotted lines joining incident rays to image
4) extend dotted lines as rays on LH side of mirror.

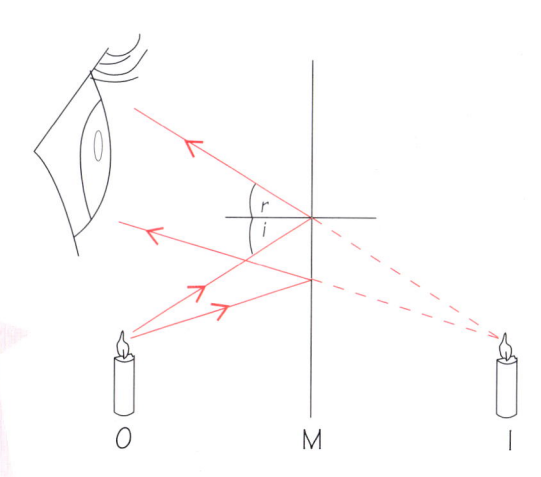

81

PHYSICAL PROCESSES

Refraction

- Less dense to more dense – direction changes.
- Direction at A – towards normal.
- Direction at B – away from normal.
- Denser medium – greater refraction.
- Refractive index – measure of refraction
  – sin *i* / sin *r*
  – about 1.5 for glass.
- Example – bottom of swimming pool appears nearer.

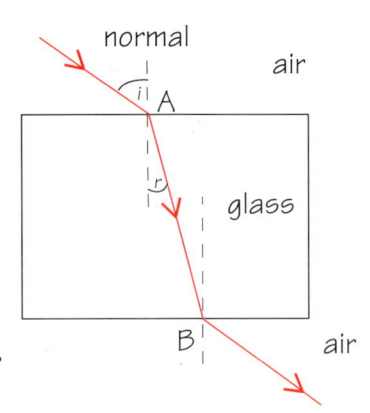

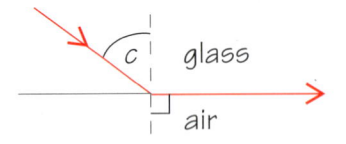

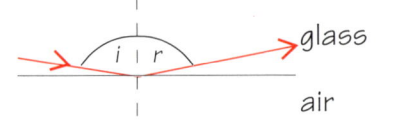

Emergent ray is parallel to incident ray.

- Critical angle *c* – light refracted at 90°.
- Incident angle greater – all light reflected back.
- This is called **total internal reflection** (TIR).
- Examples – optical fibre
  – prism binoculars.

Note that this only occurs from moving from more dense to less dense

Diffraction

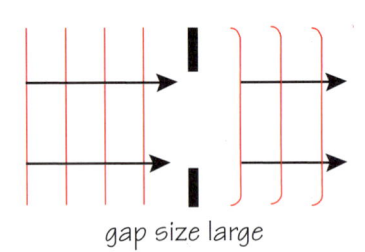

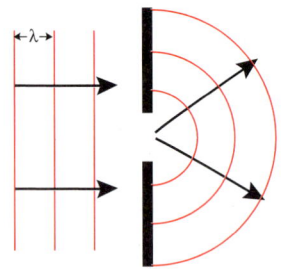

gap size large

gap same size as wavelength

- Waves spread out – past obstacle / through gap.
- Gap size – about same as wavelength.
- Examples – sound heard around corners
  – radio signals received in shadow of hills.

Electromagnetic spectrum

wavelength decreases →   ← frequency decreases

A mnemonic such as
Reading
Is
Lousy
Unless
Extremely
Good
will help to remember the order.

	Radio	Infra-red	Light	Ultra-violet	X-rays	Gamma-rays
Source	Vibrating electrons	Sun Hot bodies	Sun Luminous objects	Sun Mercury Vapour lamp	Stars X-ray tube	Radioactive substances
Detector	Radio aerial	Skin IR photographic film	Eye Photographic film	Skin (tanning) Photographic film	Photographic film	GM tube Photographic film
Use	Communication Cooking (microwaves)	Heating Remote control	Seeing Photography Photosynthesis	Security marking Fluorescent lamps	Medical photographs Astronomy	Cancer treatment

- Family of waves.
- Speed – same = 3×10^8 m/s.
- Different wavelengths – reflected, refracted, etc. differently.

82

WAVES

Radio waves

- **Transmit** – radio/TV over Earth's surface.
- **Longer wavelength** – **reflected** from ionosphere (electrically charged layer in upper atmosphere)
  – enables communication despite curvature of Earth's surface.
- **Shorter wavelength** – can penetrate ionosphere
  – used for communication with satellites
  – water molecules can strongly absorb one particular frequency so used for cooking.

Infra-red

- **Readily absorbed** – by rough, **black** surfaces.
- **Strongly reflected** – by polished, **light** surfaces.
- **Uses** – grills, toasters, radiant heaters, optical fibre communication, remote control of TV/VCR.

Light

- **Used in optical fibres** – medical endoscopes to see inside patient's body.
- **White light** – split into **colours** by prism.
- **Spectrum** – colour depends on wavelength.
- **Most refracted** – violet.
- **Least refracted** – red.
- **Brightness** – depends on **intensity/amplitude** of wave.
- **Colour filters** – **absorb** different **wavelengths** (colour subtraction).
- **Coloured objects** – behave **like** colour **filters**.

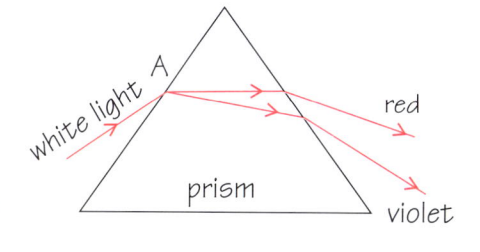

> Students often do not show the red and violet rays spreading out from point A.

Ultra-violet

- **Uses** – sunbeds/fluorescent lamps/security coding where special coating absorbs radiation and emits light.

X-radiation

- **Does not easily pass through bone/metal.**
- **Used to produce shadow pictures** of people/materials.

Gamma radiation

- **Kills harmful bacteria** in food.
- **Sterilises** surgical instruments.
- **Kills cancer cells.**

Effect on living cells

- **Microwaves** – absorbed by water in cells
  – cells may be damaged/killed by heat released.
- **Infra-red** – absorbed by skin
  – felt as heat.
- **Ultra-violet** – can pass through skin to deep tissue
  – darker skin absorbs more so less reaches deep tissue.
- **X-rays/Gamma rays** – pass through soft tissue
  – some absorbed by cells.

> Note that **high doses** of UV/X-rays/Gamma **can kill** normal cells, **lower doses** can cause cancer.

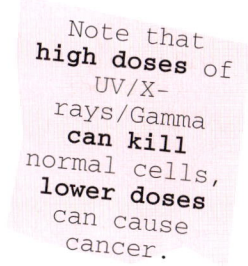

PHYSICAL PROCESSES

Sound

These are patterns seen on an oscilloscope.

- **Vibration** produces sound.
- **Examples** – guitar **string**, drum **skin**, whistle.
- **Volume** – depends on **amplitude**.
- **Pitch** – depends on **frequency**.
- **Speed** – in **air** about **340 m/s**
   – faster in **denser** substances, e.g. water
   – measure by timing **echoes**.

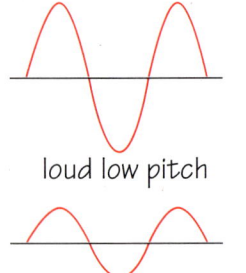

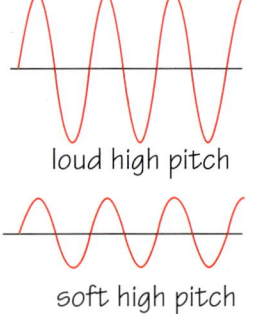

loud low pitch   loud high pitch
soft low pitch   soft high pitch

Ultrasound
- **Definition** – above **20 kHz**.
- **Reflection** – at boundary between media
   – time for detection gives distance.
- **Bats** – detect objects from echoes.
- **Sea** – measure depth
   – detect fish shoals.
- **Industry** – cleaning delicate objects
   – detect flaws in metal casings.
- **Hospital** – pre-natal scanning.

dolphins produce ultrasonic waves

Ultrasonic Scanning is thought to be safer than using X-rays; state this as a main advantage in an answer.

Seismic waves

*P comes **before** S in the alphabet – P waves arrive **before** S waves.*

- **P waves** – longitudinal
   – fast
   – travel through solids, liquids.
- **S waves** – transverse
   – slower
   – only travel through solids.
- **Refraction** – at boundary between media
   – indicates changing density.

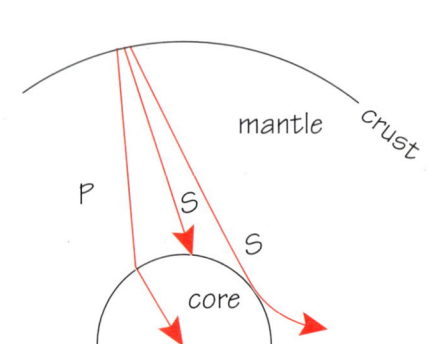

Observations suggest **Earth** – made of **layers**
   – has **thin crust**
   – has **solid mantle** with density increasing with depth
   – has core just over half Earth diameter
   – has core with liquid outer and solid inner part.

S-waves cannot pass through liquid outer core.

84

Waves Questions

1. Here is a waveform.

    (a) Measure (i) its wavelength _____ cm
    (ii) its amplitude _____ cm

    (b) It takes 0.01 s for this waveform to travel across the screen of an oscilloscope.
    Calculate (i) its frequency _____

    (ii) its speed _____

2. (a) Copy and complete the diagram to show how an image is formed in a plane mirror.

    (b) Is the image 'real' or 'virtual'? Explain your answer. _____

3. Echo location techniques can be used by a fishing trawler to find shoals of fish in the sea.
    (a) Describe how this works. _____

    (b) If the speed of sound in water is 1550 m/s and it takes 0.3 s for an echo to be received, how deep is the shoal? _____

4. Name two differences between P and S waves sent out from the epicentre of an earthquake.
    (i) _____
    (ii) _____

PHYSICAL PROCESSES

The Earth and beyond
The Solar System

Satellites

- **Moon** – **natural satellite** of Earth.
- **Sputnik** – example of **artificial satellite** – USSR 1957.
- **Use** – **beam information** to places on Earth a long way apart, e.g. TV
  - **monitor conditions** etc. on Earth, e.g. weather
  - **acts as observatory** since no interference from atmosphere.
- **Orbits** – **communication** satellite uses **high equatorial** orbit; scans same point continuously
  - **monitoring** satellite uses **low polar** orbit; scans whole N or S hemisphere each day.

There may well be a question on uses of satellites.

Orbit of communication satellite is "geostationary". time of rotation same as Earth.

Gravity

- **Attraction** – all bodies in Universe.
- **Gravitational force (g)** greater if
  - **mass** of bodies **greater**
  - **distance** apart **less**; 2 × distance = $\frac{1}{4}$ of force.
- **Earth** – $g = 10$ N/kg.
- **Larger planets**, e.g. Jupiter – **g greater**.
- **Smaller planets**, e.g. Mercury – **g smaller**.
- **Weightlessness** – **no weight**
  - **orbiting satellite**
  - **far out in space**.

An apple weighs about 1 Newton!

Orbital motion

- **Planetary orbits** – **elliptical** not circular.
- **Comets** – orbit **very elliptical**
  - much closer to Sun at times → visible.
- **Orbit larger** – **further** from Sun
  - **longer time** for orbit.
- **Small bodies**, e.g. satellites – **need certain speed** to stay in orbit.

Note that the orbit of Pluto is at an angle to those of the other planets.

*You should know the order of the planets – **M**y **V**ery **E**asy **M**ethod **J**ust **S**peeds **U**p **N**aming **P**lanets will help you!*

Solar System (not to scale)

Mercury, Venus, Earth, Mars, Jupiter, Saturn, Uranus, Neptune, Pluto

THE EARTH AND BEYOND

Universe

Stars

- **Sun** – one of millions of stars.
- **Galaxy** – group of stars
    - stars millions of times further apart than planets from Sun.
- **Universe** – at least one thousand million (billion) galaxies
    - galaxies millions of times further apart than stars.

Our galaxy (Milky Way) would look like this from space — our Sun

Life of a star

- **Birth: dust + gas** →(immense gravity)→ **star**.
- **Mass** – **very large** compared to planets.
- **Volume** – Sun (small star) million times larger volume than Earth.
- **Density** – star matter **millions of times denser than Earth** matter.
- **Heat** – stars are balls of **very hot gases**
    - creates forces tending to **expansion** of star
    - forces balance → **stability** (e.g. our Sun).
- **Size change** – **stable** for millions of years
    - expansion → **red giant** → **rapid contraction** → **supernova explosion** (if massive enough)
        - contraction → **white dwarf** (very small, cold)
        - **neutron star** (very dense) → **black hole** (no light escapes)

Make sure your answers only contain the key important points.

Energy production in a star

- **Light nuclei** – fuse → heavier nuclei
    - **vast energy release**.

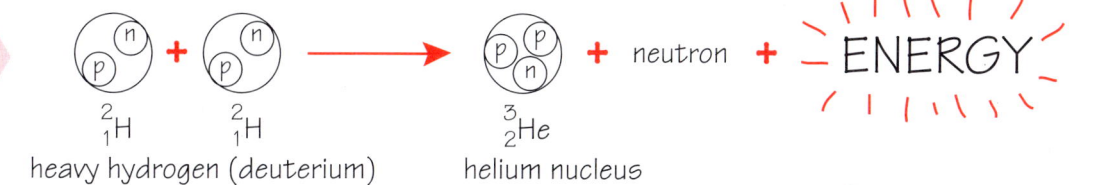

$^{2}_{1}H$ + $^{2}_{1}H$ → $^{3}_{2}He$ + neutron + ENERGY

heavy hydrogen (deuterium)   helium nucleus

Nuclear fusion is not the same process as nuclear fission (which occurs in nuclear power stations).

Origin of Universe

- **Red shift** – **light** from other galaxies **shifted to red** end of spectrum.
- **More red shift** – galaxies further away → galaxies **receding fast** → universe **expanding**.
- **Big Bang** – **theory** on possible start of universe
    - uses red shift observations
    - universe began from explosion of matter.
- **Age** – at least 15 billion years old.

Some scientists believe that the Universe has always existed – this is called the Steady State theory.

The Earth and beyond
Questions

1 One use of artificial satellites is to broadcast information around the world.

   (a) What is the name we give to this type of satellite? _____

   (b) Name and describe the use of one other type of satellite.
   _____
   _____

2 Astronauts in an orbiting spacecraft feel weightless.

   (a) What does this mean?
   _____

   (b) The spacecraft is still within the gravitational field of the Earth. Explain why the astronauts are apparently weightless.
   _____
   _____

3 Halley's comet is seen in the sky every 75 years.

   (a) With the aid of a diagram explain why it is seen only periodically and not all the time.

   (b) On your diagram draw the path of a second comet that would only ever be seen once from the Earth.

4 Describe the stages in the evolution of a star resulting in the formation of a neutron star.
   _____
   _____
   _____
   _____
   _____

Energy resources and energy transfer

Thermal energy

- Thermal energy – transferred from **hot to cold body**.

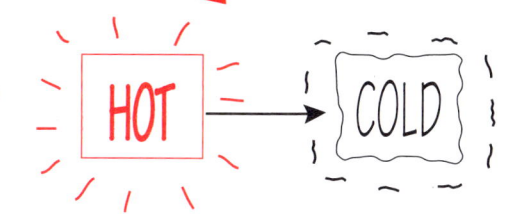

Conduction

- Adjacent particles transfer energy.
- Metal – *good conductor*
  - hotter → more kinetic energy (KE) for free electrons → **diffusion**
  - also energy transfer by collision.
- Non-metals/liquids – poor conductors.
- Gases – very poor conductors.

Convection

You should know about sources of heat loss from e.g. home, cup of tea + ways of reducing the loss by insulation.

- Gas/liquid – particles gain KE → expansion
  - hotter parts *less dense* → **rise up**
  - colder parts *more dense* → replace hotter parts.
- Examples – hot air balloon, sea breeze.

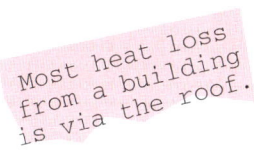

Most heat loss from a building is via the roof.

Radiation

- Energy transfer by waves.
- Part of **electromagnetic spectrum** (infra-red, IR).
- Emission – hot bodies
  - dark, matt surfaces.

Energy efficiency

$$\text{Efficiency} = \frac{\text{useful energy transferred}}{\text{total energy supplied}}$$

- Unuseful energy – wasted
  - reduces efficiency.
- Energy supplied – heats surroundings
  - increasingly **spread out**
  - more difficult to use for energy transfer.

Energy resources

- **Renewable** – will not run out, e.g. wood, tides, wind.
- **Non-renewable** – cannot be replaced, e.g. fossil fuels, nuclear.
- Power station – generates **electricity from both types**.
- Steam – produced by **non-renewable** resources + **wood/geothermal**
  - drives turbines.
- Turbines – driven directly by renewable resources
  - **solar cells** produce **electricity directly**
  - turn generators → electricity.

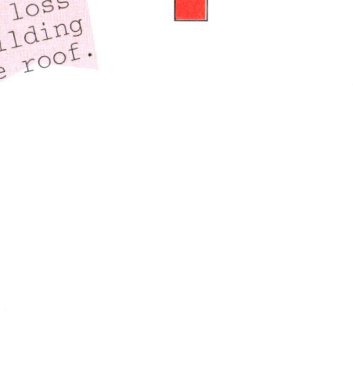

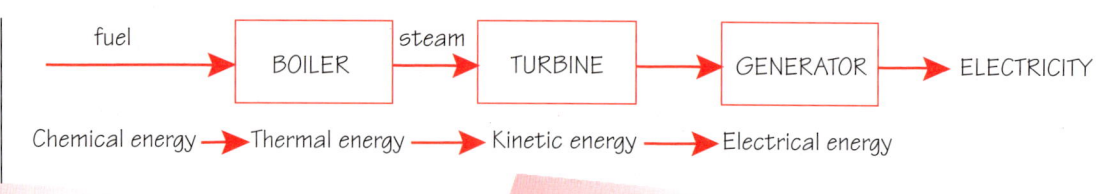

PHYSICAL PROCESSES

fuel → **BOILER** → steam → **TURBINE** → **GENERATOR** → ELECTRICITY

Chemical energy → Thermal energy → Kinetic energy → Electrical energy

Non-Renewable vs Renewable

Non-Renewable:
- Will **run out**
- **waste**
- **fuel costs**
- **transportation costs**
- **building costs high.**

Renewable:
- Will **not run out**
- **no waste**
- **no fuel costs**
- **no transportation costs**
- **Generating equipment costs high.**
(Note: above excludes wood.)

Work

Work done = force x distance
         = energy transferred

- Units – joules (J).
- 1 J – 1 Nm.

Power = work done / time taken
      = rate of energy transfer

- Units – watts (W).
- 1 W – 1 J/s.

A ramp is a machine. Machines make work easier. Other examples include: spanner, pulley, lever.

Kinetic energy (KE)

- **Moving** object has KE.
- KE depends on **mass** and **speed**.

$$KE = \frac{1}{2} \times mass \times (speed)^2$$

- Units – J.
- Example – moving car.

Students often forget that speed must be squared.

Potential energy (PE)

- **Gravitational PE** – energy stored
  – depends on **weight + height**
  – example: walking upstairs.

Gravitational PE = weight x change in vertical height

- Units – J.
- Weight depends on – mass
  – gravitational field strength, g.

Weight = mass x g

- **Gravitational field strength** – on **Earth** about **10 N/kg**
  – on **Moon** about **1.7 N/kg**.
- **Elastic PE** – energy stored
  – **depends on** change in **shape** of body
  – examples: stretched spring, catapult.

A high diver exchanges her PE for KE on the way down.

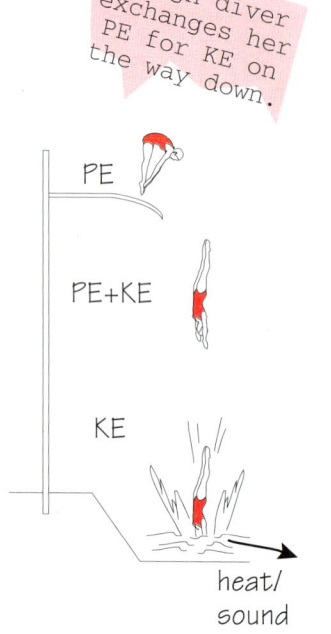

PE
PE+KE
KE
heat/sound

ENERGY RESOURCES AND ENERGY TRANSFERS

Energy resources and energy transfer
Questions

1. A 'radiator' used in home central heating should really be called a 'convector'. Do you agree? Explain your answer.

   _____
   _____

2. An electric kettle is rated at 1 kW.
   It takes 30 s to heat up a certain mass of water.
   (a) If 1 W = 1 J/s, how much energy is supplied to the kettle? _____
   _____

   (b) 10 kJ of energy is wasted. Calculate the efficiency of the kettle.
   _____

   (c) (i) How is this energy wasted? _____
   (ii) How could this waste be reduced? _____

3. (a) Name a renewable energy resource. _____
   (b) Describe three main advantages that renewable energy resources have over non-renewable resources for the generation of electricity.
   (i) _____
   (ii) _____
   (iii) _____

4. Julie runs up a staircase. Each step is 20 cm high. There are 10 steps to the top. If her weight is 450 N,
   (a) how much work must she do to reach the top?   20 cm
   _____
   _____
   _____

   (b) what power does she develop if it takes her 3 s?
   _____
   _____
   _____

PHYSICAL PROCESSES

Radioactivity
Atomic structure

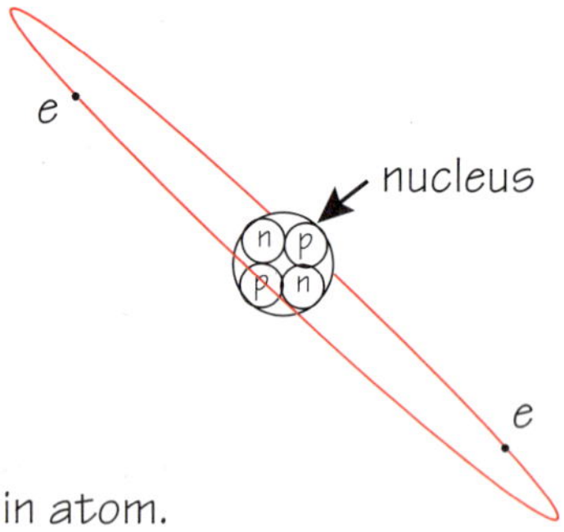

- **Atoms** – **tiny** central **nucleus** with electrons outside.
- **Radioactivity** – emitted when **nucleus changes**.
- **Nucleus** – **protons (p)** + **neutrons (n)**.
- **Electrons (e)** – **orbit** around nucleus.
- **Plum pudding model** – plums (**electrons**) **embedded** in atom.
- **Alpha scattering** → **nucleus** has positive (**+**) **charge**.

	Mass	Charge
p	1	+1
n	1	0
e	negligible	–1

Number of p = number of e overall charge on atom is zero.

Elements

- **Proton number** – **same** for atoms of **same element**.
- **Nucleon** (**mass**) **number** – total **number of p + n**.
- **Isotope** – atoms of **same element** with **different** number of **n**.
- **Radioactive isotope** – isotopes with **unstable** nuclei
  – also known as **radioisotope** or **radionuclide**.
- **Disintegration** – nuclei break up → number of **n** and **p** may change → **different element** if p changes.
- **Radiation emission** – continually
  – random.

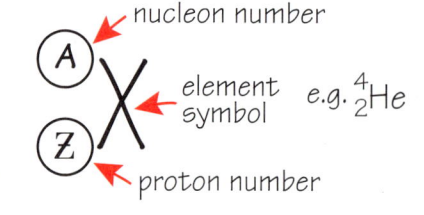

Nucleon number minus proton number gives number of neutrons.

$^A_Z X$ ← nucleon number, element symbol, proton number   e.g. $^4_2 He$

Note that γ decay has no affect on nucleon or proton number – nucleus just loses energy.

Types of radiation

Look at composition to predict new proton and nucleon numbers.

Type	Symbol	Stopped by	Composition	Charge	Mass
alpha	α	thin sheet of paper	2p + 2n (He nucleus)	+	large
beta	β	2 mm metal	electrons; n → p + e	–	tiny
gamma	γ	reduced by thick concrete / lead	Em radiation	0	0

Sources of radiation

- **Space** – cosmic rays.
- **Ground**/**building materials**.
- **Food**.
- **Medical** – radiography, e.g. chest X-ray
  – treatment, e.g. cancer.
- **Nuclear power station**.

92

RADIOACTIVITY

Dangers of radiation

- **Absorption** by material → **ionisation** of atoms.
- **Cell damage** – **may kill/cause cancer**
  - alpha source most dangerous in body
  - beta, gamma sources most dangerous outside body.

Uses of radiation

- **Monitor/control thickness** – greater absorption by thicker material
  - alpha and beta.
- **Medical treatment** – kill cancer cells
  - gamma.
- **Tracers** – trace path of fluids
  - medicine, agriculture.

GM tube measures activity.

Half-life

In practise, background count should be subtracted.

- Radioactive atoms → radiation → **stable** (non-radioactive atoms).
- **Activity decreases with time.**
- **Half-life** – **time** for activity/count rate **to halve**
  - different for different radioisotopes, e.g. Na–24 is 15 hours, Pt–239 is 24 000 years.
- **Carbon dating** – half-life 5730 years
  - used to find **age of once living radioactive materials.**

The graph shows the decay of a radionuclide. Half-life = t.

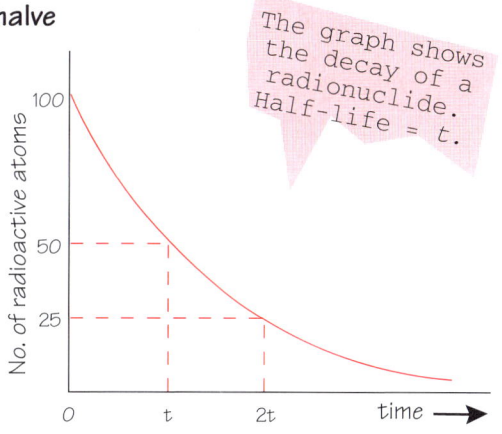

Nuclear fission

- **Neutrons** – fired at large nucleus.
- **Nucleus splits** → neutrons released → **chain reaction.**
- New atoms also radioactive.
- **Energy released** – **much larger than** associated with a chemical bond.
- Nuclear power stations release energy by nuclear fission.
- Sun releases energy by nuclear fusion.

In a nuclear power station, the chain reaction is slowed/stopped by control rods; they absorb the neutrons.

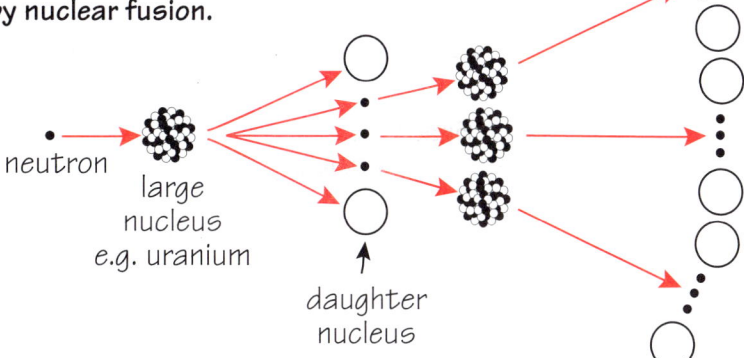

neutron → large nucleus e.g. uranium → daughter nucleus

93

PHYSICAL PROCESSES

Radioactivity
Questions

1 (a) Explain the 'plum pudding' model of the atom.

   (b) How was this model modified from the alpha scattering experiments?

2 Name two ways in which gamma radiation differs from either alpha or beta radiation.
   (a)
   (b)

3 The activity of a sample of a radionuclide was measured. It was found to be 3000 counts/min at 9 am. By 11 am this had decreased to 750 counts/min.
   (a) What instrument is used to measure the activity?

   (b) Calculate the half-life of the sample.

   (c) When the detector was moved away, the experimenter noticed that it still recorded a low count rate. Why?

4 Steel sheets are produced in a steel mill. The sheets are rolled out to a certain thickness as they pass along a conveyor belt. By drawing a diagram, explain how a radioactive source can be used to monitor and control the thickness.

Answers

Physical processes
Electricity and magnetism

1 Negative charges on rod – transfer to cloth – makes cloth –ve and rod +ve
2 (a) 6 V (b) Current through each lamp = 1.5 A, R = V/I = 6/1.5 = 4Ω
3 (a) I = P/V = 1500/250 = 6 A, Use 10 A fuse (b) 7 days @ ⅓ hour per day = 7/3 hours, Cost = 1.5 × 7/3 × 6p = 21 p   4 (a) Iron core in coil, increased number of turns, increased current (b) dc motor, loudspeaker, circuit breaker, relay, electric bell, etc.   5 (a) Output voltage bigger than input voltage (b) Number of turns needed = 7.0/2.0 × 100 = 350

Forces and motion

1 (a) Constant acceleration (b) i) Acceleration = 6/30 = 0.2 m/s² ii) distance = area under graph = area of triangle = ½ × 30 × 6 = 90 m   2 (a) Resultant force = 6500 – 850 = 5650 N; Acceleration = F/m = 5650/1200 = 4.71 m/s² (b) Reaction time, weather, condition of tyres/brakes/road
3 (a) [diagram: air drag up, weight down] (b) Constant/terminal velocity; no acceleration
4 (a) Snow skis, anything with wide flat base
(b) Area of two feet = 0.06m²
Pressure = 600/0.06 = 60 000 Pa
5 Force = 0.4/0.1 × 150 = 4 × 150 = 600 N

Waves

1 (a) (i) Wavelength = 2.75 cm (ii) Amplitude = 0.75 cm (b) (i) 1½ wavelengths fit on screen in 0.01 s; so, 1 wavelength takes ⅔ × 0.01 s; frequency = 1/ ⅔ × 0.01 = 3/0.02 = 232.5 m   (ii) Speed = 150 × 2.7 = 405 m/s
2 (a) [ray diagram of object and image in plane mirror] (b) Virtual. Not really there/cannot be projected on a screen.
3 (a) (Ultrasonic) pulse sent into water. Time to return to receiver measured. Depth of shoal = speed × time (b) 0.3 s for signal to travel there and back. Use time = 0.15s; Depth = 1550 × 0.15 = 232.5 m

4 P – longitudinal – fast – travel through solids + liquids; S – transverse – slow – travel only through solids

The Earth and beyond

1 (a) Communications satellite (b) Monitoring – gather Earth data on e.g. weather; Observatory – gather space data on e.g. planets   2 (a) No weight.
(b) Spacecraft pulled towards Earth by gravitational force; astronauts pulled towards spacecraft; floor falls away as fast as astronauts fall toward floor; no contact with floor; therefore zero weight
3 (a) Long elliptical orbit only visible when near Earth (b) Parabolic path – never returns

4 Dust + gas → star born → stability → expansion → red giant → rapid contraction → supernova → neutron star

PHYSICAL PROCESSES

Energy resources and energy transfer

1 Yes – little radiated heat – room mainly heated by creation of convection current
2 (**a**) 1kW = 1000 W; Energy supplied = 1000 × 30 s = 30000 J = 30 kJ
(**b**) Efficiency = 20 kJ/30kJ × 100 = 67 %   (**c**) (i) Heats up kettle body/surroundings; sound energy produced (ii) Insulate kettle e.g. wrap insulation around
3 (**a**) Any of wind, wave, tidal, geothermal, solar, wood (**b**) Will not run out, no waste, no fuel cost, no transportation cost   **4** (**a**) Work = force × distance = 450 × 10 × 0.2 = 900 J (**b**) Power = work done/time taken = 900/3 = 300 W

Radioactivity

1 (**a**) Plums = electrons, electrons embedded in atom (**b**) Atom has central nucleus; nucleus tiny; nucleus + ve; electrons orbit nucleus; most of atom empty space   **2** Gamma – wave not particle – no mass/charge – travels at speed of light/ 3×10^8 m/s   **3** (**a**) GM tube/counter (**b**) 9am – 3000 counts/min; 11am – 750 counts/min; therefore 2 hours → drops to ¼; 1 hour → drops to ½; half-life = 1 hour
(**c**) Recording background radiation
4 Radioactive source; source above/below sheets; detector below/above sheets; correct thickness → p counts/min recorded; thickness too big → less than p recorded; thickness too small → more than p recorded; link detector via feedback to motor; motor controls roller pressure

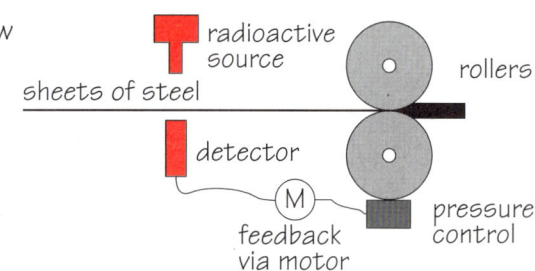